STAR WARS
MAKER LAB

STAR WARS™

MAKER LAB

Liz Lee Heinecke and Cole Horton

CONTENTS

BEFORE YOU START

THE *STAR WARS* GALAXY IS FULL OF INCREDIBLE INVENTIONS, SUPER STARSHIPS, AND FANTASTIC MOMENTS. NOW YOU CAN CREATE SOME OF THESE FOR YOURSELF, AND LEARN ABOUT REAL-WORLD SCIENCE, TOO!

The projects in this book range from easy to tricky. The quickest one can take less than an hour, while a few can take days. Once you've decided on your project, read through the step-by-step instructions carefully and make sure you have everything you need before you start.

Remember, science is a process of trial and error. If something doesn't work as you expect the first time around, make an adjustment and try again! Like all great scientists, makers, and Jedi, be ready to channel your curious, creative, and can-do spirit.

May the Force be with you.

SAFETY FIRST

All projects in this book should be approached with care, so make sure you read these safety points first!

- Always wear eye protection when handling chemicals or creating chemical reactions, including acidic liquids like vinegar.

- Keep young children (under 8 years of age), pets, and anyone not wearing eye protection away from the experimental area.

- Do not allow any chemicals to come into contact with your eyes or mouth.

- Do not use equipment that has not been recommended in the instructions.

- Do not eat or drink while creating a project.

- Be careful when using paint or food coloring as they can stain surfaces and clothing.

- Wash your hands and clean all equipment when you have finished your project.

 If you see this symbol it means that you will need to ask an adult for help or supervision with the step. Take particular care when using sharp objects like scissors, craft knives, pins, strong glue, or cooking equipment.

IMPORTANT NOTE TO PARENTS

The projects in this book may require adult help and supervision, depending on your child's age and ability. Always ensure that your child uses tools that are appropriate to their age, and offer help and supervision as necessary to keep them safe. The publisher cannot accept any liability for injury, loss, or damage to any property or user following suggestions in this book.

HOW TO USE THE TEMPLATES

For some of the more complicated projects, this book includes templates on pages 120 to 125 to help you achieve the perfect shapes for your projects. If you need to use a template, the instructions will tell you which page to find it on. When you're on that page, lay tracing paper onto the template and trace over its outline with a sharp pencil. Then turn the tracing paper over and place it on the material you wish to cut out. Trace over the shape on the back of the tracing paper with the pencil. When you lift the paper up, you will see the pencil marks have been transferred to your material. Now you can cut out the shape.

WHERE TO GET YOUR SUPPLIES

Most of the supplies, ingredients, and equipment used in this book are easy-to-find household products. Everything else can be purchased online or at your local hardware, department, stationery, or grocery store. Please ask an adult before purchasing anything.

WHY NOT TRY?

Many projects in this book include a "Why not try?" section. This will show you alternative models from the *Star Wars* galaxy that you can create or suggest different ways to decorate the models to make them extra special.

DIFFICULTY
Easy

LIGHTSABER DUEL

FACE YOUR ENEMY IN A JEDI BATTLE

The lightsaber is an energy sword with a glowing plasma blade used by the Jedi and some of their enemies. Crafting a lightsaber is a special trial that every Jedi apprentice must complete. Using a penlight and some water, you too can see what it's like to wield a lightsaber.

Tiny milk particles in the water reflect the penlight's light.

IN A GALAXY FAR, FAR AWAY....

Each lightsaber is as unique as its owner. However, they all share common elements, such as a handle, emitter, and power switch. They are powered by rare, colorful gems called kyber crystals, which bond with Force-attuned users. A lightsaber can cut through most materials and even deflect Force lightning.

Kylo Ren's crossguard lightsaber

WHAT YOU NEED

Jug and enough water
to fill your container

Penlight (one per lightsaber)

Scissors

Sticky tape

Milk

Silver tape

Colored
cellophane

Clear container with flat sides

Colored cellophane
gives color to the
beam of light.

1

Firstly, personalize your penlight with silver tape. Every Jedi designs his or her own handle, so each one is unique. The ideal penlight for this experiment shines a narrow but strong beam.

2

These lightsabers get their color from cellophane rather than kyber crystals. Tape some onto the sides of your tank. You could use two colors—blue for the light side and red for the dark side!

HOW IT WORKS

LIGHT WAVES

Light waves carry energy that our eyes detect as a spectrum of colors. The colors we see depend on which waves are reflected or absorbed. Grass appears green because most of the light waves that hit it are absorbed except for green ones, which are reflected back at our eyes.

WHY MILK?

Light waves from penlights are hard to see, until they hit a solid surface, or are reflected by particles. By adding milk to water, the tiny milk droplets bounce the light back into our eyes, making the beam visible.

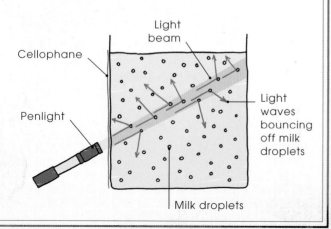

Light beam

Cellophane

Light waves bouncing off milk droplets

Penlight

Milk droplets

Luke Skywalker's lightsaber

n Skywalker's lightsaber

Mace Windu's lightsaber

Darth Sidious's lightsaber

Darth Vader's lightsaber

3

Position the tank on a flat surface with space to move about at each end. Once it's in the right spot, fill the tank with water—you won't want to shift it once it is full!

4

Next, add just a drop of milk to the water and stir gently until it disappears. Be sure to add just a tiny drop at a time—you can always add more milk later if you need to.

WHY NOT TRY?

The color of a lightsaber is determined by the kyber crystal inside it. Jedi lightsabers are often green or blue, while Mace Windu wields a rare purple blade. Sith lightsabers are always red. Try different colored cellophane to see which color best suits you.

IN OUR GALAXY...

LASER LIGHT SHOWS

Fog and smoke machines are often used so you can see laser light beams. Much like the milk added to water, the tiny particles in fog and smoke reflect the laser light making it more visible at concerts and events.

5 Now shine your penlight through the tank. You should be able to see the beam of your lightsaber in the water. If you can't, add another drop of milk and try again.

6 Shine a penlight through each sheet of cellophane. See how the beams differ from each other? Be careful not to hold the penlights too close to the cellophane as it can get hot and melt.

OH MY!
Goodness me, humans are terribly fragile, not like droids. So don't shine your penlight in anyone's eyes.

"THIS IS THE WEAPON OF A JEDI KNIGHT."
Obi-Wan Kenobi

7

Now it's time to challenge a friend to a duel! For best results, conduct your battle in a darkened room. Why not film it, too? You could even try making lightsaber sound effects!

YOU'VE DONE IT!

On Cloud City, Luke Skywalker bravely battles Darth Vader in a fierce lightsaber duel.

ATTACK OR DEFENSE?

Traditionally, lightsabers are the weapon of the Jedi, used for defense rather than attack. However, General Grievous collects lightsabers from Jedi he has defeated and can use four at a time to attack his enemies!

DIFFICULTY
Tricky

DEATH STAR TRACTOR BEAM

SNARE A STARSHIP WITH MAGNETS

Across the galaxy, tractor beams use invisible force fields to push or pull objects in space. When caught in a tractor beam's grasp, it is very hard to get away. The Death Star uses an array of tractor beams to capture starships like the *Millennium Falcon*. You too can move objects without touching them by using strong magnets.

WHAT YOU NEED

Newspaper

Measuring cup

Tall glass

Ruler

PVA glue

Paint

Bowl

Paintbrush

2 strong magnets

Pencil

Permanent marker

Craft knife

Balloon

Scissors

Strong tape

Masking tape

Needle and thread

Cardboard egg carton

Glue gun

IN A GALAXY FAR, FAR AWAY....

The DS-1 Orbital Battle Station, better known as the Death Star, is equipped with more than 700 tractor beam emitters. These emitters create invisible force fields that can snare smaller ships. The tractor beams are so powerful they can not only stop a ship in its tracks, but also pull it into the space station's hangar for inspection.

The *Millennium Falcon*'s sublight engines can be created simply using paint.

1

To construct your papier-mâché Death Star use a ruler to tear newspaper pages into strips around 1 inch thick. You'll need lots of strips so tear enough for a big pile!

2

Blow up the balloon. Mix 2 cups PVA glue with 1 cup water in a bowl. Coat the newspaper strips with this paste and "paint" them onto the balloon, building up several layers.

HOW IT WORKS

MAGNETIC FIELDS

Magnets are made of ferromagnetic metals such as nickel and iron. These metals produce invisible magnetic fields that attract or repel other magnetic objects.

PUSH AND PULL

A magnet has two ends called poles: a north and a south pole. Opposite poles attract one another, while like poles push each other away. Your *Millennium Falcon* model will swing around until the magnet inside is drawn to the opposite pole of the magnet in the Death Star.

Magnetic fields: opposite poles attract

South pole

North pole

Magnets

WHY NOT TRY?

Tractor beams are used by a wide variety of spacecraft, from Republic tugboats to Imperial Star Destroyers. You could use magnets to recreate the dramatic moment Darth Vader's *Devastator* captures the *Tantive IV* in its tractor beam.

Devastator

Tantive IV

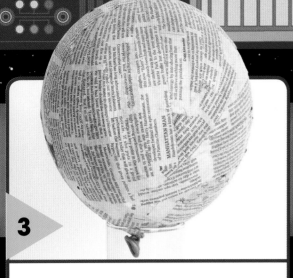

3

Place your papier-mâché balloon on a glass for a few hours to dry. Tap the balloon to test when it is dry. Cover any holes with a second coat of newspaper and paste.

4

When your sphere is dry, paint it gray, covering the newspaper thoroughly. Trace around a drinking glass to make a small circle over the spot where the balloon is tied.

IN OUR GALAXY...

COLLECTING ON MARS

Scientists designed special "capture magnets" for the Mars Exploration Rover robots. These magnets collected magnetic dust particles from the Red Planet's surface and atmosphere for analysis. Data from these particles helps us learn more about the elements that make up the surface and atmosphere of Mars.

5

Ask an adult to cut a circle out of the balloon following the traced line. Remove the popped balloon from inside the sphere and place it in the trash. Keep the circle for later.

OH MY!
You need a sharp knife to cut the circle, so ask an adult to do this for you.

Experiment with folding and rolling construction paper to create these famous starships.

6

Next, install your "tractor beam" magnet. Place a strong magnet inside the sphere near the hole you've just made and stick it down firmly with strong tape.

7

Carefully poke two tiny holes in the globe with a needle, a few inches away from the large hole. Then string some thread through these holes, to hang your Death Star.

"WE'RE CAUGHT IN A TRACTOR BEAM. IT'S PULLING US IN!"
Han Solo

You need to use a glue gun for this step, so ask an adult to help.

10

To create the *Millennium Falcon*, cut out two egg cups from an egg carton to make two disks and two folded pieces. These will be the top, bottom, and forward mandibles of the ship.

11

Magnet

Mandibles

Use a glue gun to glue the folded pieces to the bottom disk and glue a magnet inside the ship. String a thread through the top disk of the ship and glue it onto the bottom disk.

8 Turn over the papier-mâché circle you previously cut out and place it back into the hole. Tape it in place and paint over it in gray. This will become the Death Star's superlaser dish.

9 Color a length of masking tape with a black permanent marker and cut a thin strip of it. Run the strip around the center of the sphere. This gives you a line to follow for your decorations.

ULTIMATE POWER

The Death Star is the ultimate weapon. Constructed by the Galactic Empire, this moon-sized battle station can destroy entire planets with its kyber crystal-powered superlaser. As such, it is a mighty symbol of the Emperor's authority and is feared throughout the galaxy.

Antenna

Laser cannon

Cockpit

12 If you want to make your ship look more like the *Millennium Falcon*, use the carton to build a cockpit, laser cannons, and antenna. Then paint it with as much detail as you like.

13 Hang or hold the Death Star with the thread. Swing the *Falcon* using its own thread around the Death Star until it is pulled in by magnetic forces.

YOU'VE DONE IT!

KYBER CRYSTALS

GROW YOUR OWN SUGAR CRYSTALS

Rare kyber crystals form in remote caves across the galaxy. Kyber crystals are attuned to the Force, and are used by the Jedi and the Sith to make their lightsabers. You can create your own colored sugar crystals in your kitchen, but you'll need to be patient because your crystals will take a few days to "grow."

WHAT YOU NEED

Sugar

4 wooden skewers

Measuring cup

5 tall glasses

4 clothespins

Food coloring

Spatula (heat-resistant)

Saucepan filled with 1 cup of cold water

You will also need a stove.

The above ingredients make enough solution for 4 sugar crystals.

START HERE

1

Your crystals will grow out of a strong sugar solution. Pour 1 cup of water and 4 cups of sugar into a saucepan on the stove. With an adult's help, turn the stove to high.

IN A GALAXY FAR, FAR AWAY....

Precious kyber crystals are essential in the construction of lightsabers. These Force-attuned gems supply lightsabers with energy and color, and create a special and deep bond between the blade and its user.

OH MY!
Almost-boiling sugar syrup?! Make sure you find an adult to help you.

2

As the water gets hotter, gently stir the mixture with a spatula, and watch out for hot splashes! Soon the sugar will start to dissolve, but keep stirring until the sugar has disappeared.

3

Heat the sugary water for around 3 minutes until it's very hot, but not boiling. If bubbles rise to the surface, turn the heat down. Once you have a syrupy liquid, turn off the heat.

Repeat this step for each skewer and set them aside.

4 Let your sugar solution cool down for around 10 minutes and then pour it into the measuring cup. Wait a little longer if you're not sure—very hot liquid could crack the glass.

5 Now pour 1 cup of sugar into a tall glass. Dip a skewer into the sugar solution and then into the sugar in the glass. This creates a coating of granules for your crystals to grow on.

HOW IT WORKS

MIXING MOLECULES

Each sugar granule is a tiny crystal made of trillions of molecules bonded together. When you mix sugar with hot water, the sugar molecules break apart and combine with water molecules to form what scientists call a "supersaturated" solution.

STICKY SUGAR

As the solution cools, some sugar molecules are attracted to the sugar crystals coating the skewer. They snap on like jigsaw pieces, making the crystals grow bigger and bigger.

As more molecules attach to the skewer, your crystal grows.

Wooden skewer

Sugar molecule

Sugar solution

Sugar crystals

Water molecule

6

Next, carefully pour a small amount of food coloring into each of your four empty glasses. You could use different food coloring in each glass to create different colored crystals.

7

Next, fill up each of the four glasses with the cool sugar solution and stir.

WHY NOT TRY?
What color crystals will you create? If you want to be a Jedi Knight turn your crystals blue, green, or purple. Make them red if you'd prefer to be a Sith. Other colors you could choose include the Jedi Temple Guards' rare yellow blades, Sabine Wren's black Darksaber, and Ahsoka Tano's white blades.

IN OUR GALAXY...

A TOUCH OF FROST

Just as sugar and water molecules mix together in this experiment, water molecules mix with oxygen molecules in the air to form water vapor. In cold weather, damp air can form an icy coating called "hoar frost." This frost clings to and grows on any exposed surface, including trees, window panes, and wires.

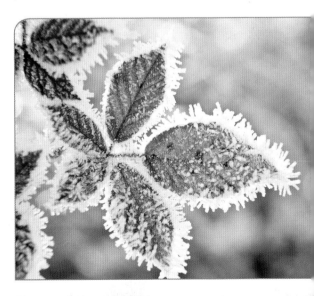

8 Put the skewer into the liquid, holding it in place with a clothespin. Don't let the skewer touch the bottom. Sugar molecules will begin sticking to the sugar granules on the skewer.

Use two clothespins if the glass is too big for one.

9 Leave your glasses for several days in a safe place. If a sugar crust forms on top of the solution, gently break the crust and remove it—this will allow the crystals to keep growing.

After facing a series of trials, Ezra Bridger is rewarded with his own kyber crystal. Now he can follow in the footsteps of all Jedi Knights and build his own lightsaber.

POWERFUL GEMS

At the core of all lightsabers lies the secret of their power: kyber crystals. These amazing gems are colorless until they are "awoken" by a Force user. The crystals work naturally with the light side of the Force, and are often used in blue and green lightsabers. However, a dark side user corrupts the crystal and turns it red.

Jedi Kanan Jarrus needs all his skills and training to take on the Grand Inquisitor and his double-bladed red lightsaber.

10

Once your sugar crystals are large enough, remove each skewer from the glass. Your colorful crystals are now fully grown! Place them on a plate to dry and don't be tempted to eat them!

YOU'VE DONE IT!

CRACKED CRYSTAL

Kylo Ren's red lightsaber contains a cracked kyber crystal. This creates instability in the lightsaber, causing power to leak out in the form of two smaller "blades" near the handle.

"THE HEART OF THE LIGHTSABER, THE CRYSTAL IS."
YODA

JABBA SLIME

MAKE SOME OOZY GREEN GOO

Jabba the Hutt is a vile creature. This monstrous crime lord is famous for his terrible temper, horrible habits, and for leaving a slimy trail of terror across the galaxy. Here's how to make your own gangster gloop using just a few simple ingredients.

You can make more than one batch of slime to make it stretch even further.

> "IF I TOLD YOU HALF THE THINGS I'VE HEARD ABOUT JABBA THE HUTT, YOU'D PROBABLY SHORT-CIRCUIT."
>
> C-3PO to R2-D2

IN A GALAXY FAR, FAR AWAY.....

Jabba the Hutt rules his criminal empire from his palace on Tatooine. Don't get him angry, or you could be fed to his pet monster, the rancor, or worse, the terrifying sarlacc.

WHAT YOU NEED

Teaspoon

Tablespoon

PVA glue

Contact lens solution (contains boric acid, but not hydrogen peroxide)

Cup or bowl

Food coloring

Baking soda

START HERE

1

Start by pouring about around ¼ cup of PVA glue into a bowl. PVA glue contains polyvinyl acetate, a chemical made up of molecule chains, which is perfect for making slime.

2

Add a quarter of a teaspoon of baking soda to the PVA glue. Baking soda is also known as sodium bicarbonate, or bicarbonate of soda, and is used to make cakes, pancakes, and bread.

HOW IT WORKS

LET'S STICK TOGETHER

Glue is made up of molecules linked together in long, repeating chains called polymers. In PVA glue, these polymers slide around freely until you add a chemical known as a crosslinker, which makes them stick together.

MAKING A CONNECTION

The crosslinking chemical in this Jabba slime experiment is made by mixing the baking soda with the contact lens solution. The crosslinker connects the polymer chains in the glue to create super sticky green goo.

Molecule

Polymer (glue)

Crosslinker

RATHTARS

These dangerous, tentacled, and slimy creatures hunt in packs. Known for their extreme aggression, rathtars are themselves sought by hunters and collectors across the galaxy.

3

Next, mix the PVA glue and baking soda together with a spoon. Stir the mixture thoroughly to make sure that it is smooth. Keep stirring until all the lumps have disappeared.

WHY NOT TRY?
You can make your slime any color you like. Why not use different food coloring to create blue, orange, or even glittery slime.

Blue Gungan slobber

Orange and yellow rathtar tentacle goo

Yellow and green glitter dianoga slime

DIANOGA

The weird, slime-oozing dianoga lives in the Death Star's trash compactor. It feeds on garbage and anything else that falls into its home.

IN OUR GALAXY...

PLASTIC FANTASTIC

Plastics are polymers. Light and durable, plastic is used every day to protect food, create textiles, build houses, and make hundreds of car parts.

VOYAGE TO MARS

A polymer called polyethylene is used in plastic bags. However, scientists at NASA are creating polyethylene plastics that are tougher and lighter than aluminum. They hope these polymers can one day help astronauts travel safely to Mars.

Keep slime far away from furniture and carpets as it could stain them!

4

To make your slime more Jabba-like, stir through a few drops of green food coloring until it is mixed fully. The more green food coloring you use, the greener the slime.

5

Add one tablespoon of contact lens solution to the green liquid. This acts as the crosslinking chemical. Keep on stirring the mixture until it firms up and turns into a glob of slime.

COUNCIL OF CRIMINALS

Jabba is a member of the Hutt species. Hutts are large, slug-like creatures from the planet Nal Hutta. This Outer Rim world is covered in hot, stinking swamps. It is from here that the Grand Hutt Council controls a galaxy-wide crime organization. They are wealthy and powerful but it's never enough. The Hutts remain greedy, selfish, and sneaky.

6 If your slime looks and feels too sticky, you could add more contact lens solution to the mixture. When it is ready, remove the glob from the mixing container.

7 Now you can play with your slime! After you have finished, store the slime in an airtight container or throw it away. Then make sure you wash your hands thoroughly.

YOU'VE DONE IT!

FRESH SNACK
A Hutt's favorite snack is a juicy gorg, eaten alive in a single gulp.

Gobbling down gorgs, paddy frogs, and slime pods gives Jabba very bad breath. Princess Leia finds this out the hard way when she's taken prisoner by the villain.

DIFFICULTY
Medium

GALACTIC PLANETS

CREATE COLORFUL COSMIC EGGS

Get ready to jump through hyperspace on an exciting interplanetary mission! Travel to the Outer Rim and back to discover the amazing planets that many weird and wonderful species call home. Use food coloring, vinegar, and eggs to create your own solar system of beautiful, sandy, or even fiery, planets.

IN A GALAXY FAR, FAR AWAY....

From a distance, planets can look many different colors. These colors are clues to what you may find there. This blue planet is likely to be a world of water. It could be home to underwater cities and creatures that live in water.

Red planets might be volcanic. They may be too hot to set foot on!

Turn the egg around for the best view of your planet.

Yellow patches on a planet may be vast, sandy deserts.

Green planets are often covered in forests and swamps.

WHAT YOU NEED

Hard-boiled eggs in a bowl

Vinegar

Tablespoon

Plastic gloves

Plate

Chopstick or toothpick

Shallow container

Food coloring (neon, if you can get it)

Whipped cream

Paper towel

Wear something to protect your eyes when handling vinegar.

START HERE

1

Ask an adult to hard boil some eggs for you. Once cooled, put the eggs into a bowl and cover them completely with vinegar. Soak for five minutes.

2

While your eggs are soaking, spray a layer of whipped cream into your container. You can cover the bottom completely or just use a section.

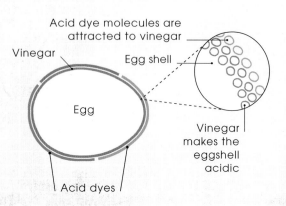

Green and black

Red and black

WHY NOT TRY?

Below are some planets from the *Star Wars* universe that can be used as inspiration for your eggs. You could also use your imagination to make up your own distant worlds!

HOW IT WORKS

VINEGAR BATH

Most food coloring depends on acid to help it stick to different surfaces. This type of food coloring is known as an acid dye. When you soak an egg in vinegar—a mild acid—a thin coating stays on the shell. This creates an acidic environment for the food coloring to bond with, dyeing the egg with amazing colour swirls.

Acid dye molecules are attracted to vinegar

Vinegar

Egg shell

Egg

Vinegar makes the eggshell acidic

Acid dyes

MON CALA

Home of the Mon Calamari and Quarren, this Outer Rim planet is almost entirely covered by water.

BESPIN

A gas giant, the planet Bespin has a thin layer of atmosphere. Within that layer floats Cloud City.

MUSTAFAR

Volcanoes erupt constantly on this lava-covered planet. Many criminals have their hideaways on Mustafar.

TOYDARIA

Inhabited by the flying Toydarian species, this world of forests and swamps is ruled by a wise, kind king.

3

Use the back of a tablespoon to smooth down the whipped cream in the container. This will keep the pattern for your egg nice and even.

4

Now it's time to create your planet's surface and unique colors! Drip food coloring over the whipped cream. You could try small drops or big splashes.

Green and yellow

Blue and black

IN OUR GALAXY...

DECORATIVE DYES

Acid dyes are used to color fabrics that are made from animal products like wool and silk. The clothes you are wearing right now could have been colored in this way!

NAL HUTTA
Homeworld of the slug-like Hutt species, this planet is covered in stinking, marshy bogs.

DAGOBAH
Swampy but full of life, Dagobah is the refuge of Jedi Master Yoda. He trains Luke Skywalker here.

NABOO
This beautiful world is known for its grassy plains and clear blue oceans. The Naboo and Gungans live here.

DATHOMIR
Witches rule this gloomy, misty planet. They draw from the planet's dark energy to perform strange magic.

5

Use as many different colors as you like to decorate your egg planet. Once you are happy with your color mix, swirl the colors together using a chopstick or toothpick.

6

Use a spoon to lift the eggs out of the vinegar. Rub them gently but firmly with a paper towel to remove the outer layer and reveal the lighter shell beneath.

Just after he turns to the dark side, Anakin travels to the lava planet Mustafar.

"CLEAR YOUR MINDS AND FIND OBI-WAN'S WAYWARD PLANET, WE WILL."
Yoda to Younglings

You can put different colors in the tray for each egg.

7

Roll the eggs through the food coloring until they are completely coated. Wear plastic gloves to stop the color staining your hands. Put your colorful eggs on a plate to dry.

8

When the eggs are dry, your planets are complete! What type of planets are they? What are they called? What beautiful or beastly creatures can be found there?

YOU'VE DONE IT!

STAR SYSTEMS IN THE *STAR WARS* GALAXY

The galaxy is filled with millions of planets, moons, and more than 400 billion stars. The stars provide heat and light for the countless species that live here. The galaxy spans several thousand light years from the Core to the Outer Rim, a mysterious region that few have dared to explore.

Core   Colonies

Mid Rim

Expansion Region   Outer Rim

***STAR WARS* GALAXY MAP**

BUSY WORKER DROIDS

BUILD YOUR OWN ROVING BRISTLEBOT

DIFFICULTY
Tricky

The Empire may rule the galaxy, but it's droids that keep it running. If a job needs doing, there's a robot designed to do it, whether it's flying a starship, engaging enemies, or performing surgery. Here's how to make a robot of your own with a basic circuit. Watch it spin and scuttle—rather like a certain droid named after a mouse!

A paper cover can be put over your bristlebot so it looks like a mouse droid.

WHAT YOU NEED

Scrubbing brush

Metallic pen

Zip tie

2 AA batteries

Insulated wire with crocodile clips

Battery holder

 Vibrating motor

Scissors

Black construction paper   Ruler   Electrical tape

Double-sided tape

START HERE

1

Your bristlebot will get its power from the vibrating motor. Attach it securely to one end of the brush handle with a zip tie or tape, ensuring it can spin without hitting the brush.

Simplified paper version of a mouse droid's communication system.

IN A GALAXY FAR, FAR AWAY....

Tiny mouse droids, also known as MSE-6 droids, scuttle around the Death Star cleaning floors, making repairs, delivering messages, and guiding troops.

OH MY!
I can't abide malfunctioning droids. Ask an adult for help to make your robot.

2

Now it's time to add the battery holder. This must be placed near the motor. Attach it to the brush, leaving enough space to insert the batteries. Stick it down firmly with double-sided tape.

3

Place both AA batteries in the holder. Match the + and – markings on the battery holder with those on the batteries to make sure the batteries are placed in the correct way.

4

Start connecting your circuit. Attach a wire from the battery holder to the motor, twisting it firmly around one of the motor's metal loops. Put electrical tape over the top to secure it.

5

Next, take the other wire from the battery holder. Secure the metal part of it inside one of the crocodile clips on the insulated wire. Your circuit is nearly complete.

HOW IT WORKS

ENERGETIC ELECTRONS

All things are made of tiny building blocks called atoms. These atoms contain electrons, which carry an electrical charge. Some materials, like the metal inside wires, are called electrical conductors. They create paths for the flow of electrons.

COMPLETING THE CIRCLE

The wires in your robot create a complete circuit through which electricity can flow. As it flows, it powers a motor and makes it spin. As the motor spins, it creates vibrations that travel through the brush and into the bristles. The bristles shake, making the robot move.

Electrical load
(like a light bulb
or a motor)

Wire that
conducts
electrons

Power source
(such as a battery)

WHY NOT TRY?
You can decorate your bristlebot to look like anything. What about making a paper cover shaped like one of these useful droids?

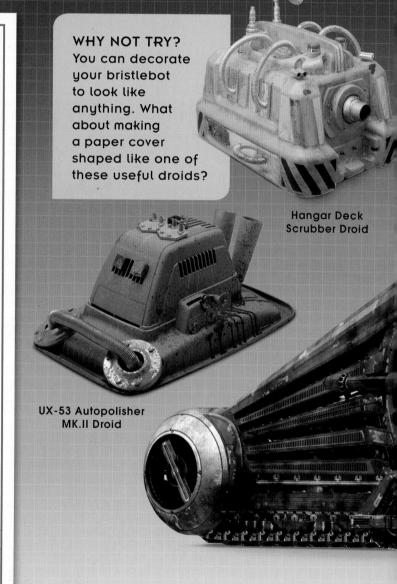

Hangar Deck
Scrubber Droid

UX-53 Autopolisher
MK.II Droid

6 The last thing you want is your droid tripping up on stray wires. Wind any long wires around the base or handle of the brush, or tape them down so they don't get in the way.

7 Grip your brush firmly, but don't touch the motor. Attach the unused crocodile clip to the empty metal loop on the motor and get ready for vibrations as the motor turns on!

Build papier-mâché around a balloon or bowl to create a dome shape.

LIN Demolition Autonomous
Mine Layer Droid

GTAW-74 Welder Droid

Use a large brush to make this mean-looking tank droid.

NR-N99 Tank Droid

IN OUR GALAXY...

SHINING BRIGHT

The circuit in your bristlebot is similar to those in many electrical objects. This flashlight is powered by batteries connected to a light bulb by metal strips. When the switch is on, the circuit is complete so the bulb glows. When the switch is in the off position, it creates a break in the circuit, stopping the flow of electrons.

Never touch the motor while it's spinning.

8

Place your bot on a flat surface, let go, and watch it work! To stop it, break the circuit by carefully undoing a crocodile clip. Don't leave it running for too long as the motor may get hot.

9

Now your droid has the moves, it's time for it to look the part, too. Why not make a mouse-droid shell using construction paper and the template from page 121.

MECHANICAL MOUSE

Mouse droids zip around the Death Star's dark corridors, keeping life aboard the space station running smoothly.

Each mouse droid is programmed with only one skill, so they often work together in packs. This means that if you spot one, there will usually be more to follow.

Chopper and AP-5 sneak into an Imperial security outpost in disguise. Chopper argues with a mouse droid, which answers back in beeps and squeaks.

10

Once you have decorated the shell, switch your mouse droid on, slip the cover over the top, and watch it scoot around. You could even use your droid to carry messages for you!

YOU'VE DONE IT!

"THE EMPIRE NEVER DID TAKE DROIDS SERIOUSLY."
AP-5

SCAREDY MICE

Teeny-tiny mouse droids aren't built for fighting. When one sees Chewbacca, it shrieks and scurries away in fear!

MUSTAFAR VOLCANO

CONSTRUCT YOUR OWN VOLCANO

On the edge of the galaxy lies the planet Mustafar. This nightmarish world is home to some of the galaxy's most fiendish villains, such as Sith Lord Darth Vader. Mustafar is covered with volcanoes, forever spewing out molten lava. You can create your own volcanic eruption using vinegar, baking soda, and food coloring.

Red and orange food coloring creates realistic-looking lava.

WHAT YOU NEED

Ruler

Plastic bottle   Vinegar

PVA glue

Baking soda   Food coloring

Tablespoon

Scissors

Parcel tape

Newspaper

Bowl

Paintbrush

IN A GALAXY FAR, FAR AWAY....

Far off in the Outer Rim, the fiery planet of Mustafar is a frightening place. Its surface is covered with craggy rocks and red-hot lava. It is so inhospitable that only the villains with the most to hide will base themselves here.

Volcanoes come in different shapes. You can make your volcano as steep or as flat as you wish.

START HERE

Cutting into the bottle is tricky, so ask an adult for help.

1

Using a pair of scissors, carefully cut the top off your plastic bottle. The plastic edge will be sharp, so take care. The lower part of the bottle will form the main vent of your volcano.

2

Stick the bottle to the center of the black cardboard with the open end at the top. Use five or six pieces of parcel tape stuck all the way around to make sure the bottle is secure.

3 Scrunch up newspaper into lots of evenly sized balls. Use the parcel tape to stick these balls around the outside of the bottle to form the volcano's basic shape.

4 Now it is time to cover the volcano with papier-mâché. Mix 2 cups of PVA glue with 1 cup of water. Stir until your mixture is a fairly smooth paste.

Obi-Wan Kenobi and Anakin Skywalker battle each other in a spectacular lightsaber duel above Mustafar's blazing lava fields.

CAVE DWELLERS

Mustafar's main insect-like species, the Mustafarians, live in underground caves. Here they are safely protected from the rivers of lava and intense heat above ground. The caves are made by Mustafar's native, heat-resistant lava fleas as they feed on the planet's crust.

Mustafarians ride on the huge lava fleas to move around the scorching surface of their planet.

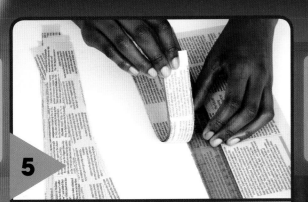

5

Use a ruler to tear the rest of your newspaper into many equal-sized strips. Tear the strips across the page, so they are short—this will make them easier to stick on.

6

With a paintbrush, cover both sides of the newspaper strips with a thick coating of the PVA and water mixture. Do this on top of a spare piece of newspaper so you don't make a mess.

7

Stick the strips onto your volcano. Some should overlap the rim of the bottle. Build up layers until you're happy with the shape. Leave to dry.

"...MUSTAFAR IS WHERE JEDI GO TO DIE."
Hera Syndulla

8

Once dry, paint the model with a base coat of white paint, and then black. Use red paint to create rivers of lava flowing down the sides. Leave to dry.

9 Place your dry, finished model on a tray or surface that cannot be stained. Measure out a ¼ cup of baking soda and tip it into the bottle inside your volcano.

10 Add several drops of red food coloring and two tablespoons of water to the baking soda. Stir the mixture thoroughly with a spoon. Your lava is now ready and waiting.

HOW IT WORKS

IT'S A GAS

Chemical reactions occur when different chemicals mix together. The molecules change, forming new bonds to create new substances, which are known as products. One of the products of the reaction between baking soda and vinegar is carbon dioxide gas (the other product is salt). Gas pressure builds up within the bottle inside your volcano, causing carbon dioxide bubbles to spill out like lava.

Vinegar

Chemical reaction →

Baking soda + Water

Carbon dioxide gas + Water + Salt

11 Ready for the eruption? Measure out 1 cup of vinegar and carefully pour about half of this into your volcano. Watch what happens as it combines with the baking soda mixture inside.

12 Your volcano will "erupt" as the baking soda mixture reacts with the vinegar. Keep pouring the rest of the vinegar slowly inside until the volcano stops erupting.

YOU'VE DONE IT!

Mustafarians and their trusty DLC-13 mining droids harvest valuable minerals from the planet's lava.

IN OUR GALAXY...

UNDER PRESSURE

In active volcanoes, pressure builds under the Earth's crust until the volcano erupts, spewing out lava, ash, and hot gas.

RING OF FIRE

There are thought to be more than 1,500 active volcanoes today. Many of these are located around the edges of the Pacific Ocean in a region known as the Ring of Fire. The Ring is 25,000 miles long, and contains more than 400 active and dormant volcanoes. Mount Kilauea, on the island of Hawaii, has been constantly erupting since 1983.

WHY NOT TRY?
Did you know that lava can sometimes appear blue at dawn or dusk as volcanic sulfur gases catch fire on contact with the air?

You could create truly amazing-colored lava by using different food coloring.

ANAKIN'S MECHNO-ARM

BUILD YOUR OWN ARTIFICIAL ARM

After losing an arm in a fierce lightsaber duel with the villainous Count Dooku, Jedi Anakin Skywalker supervises the construction of a superior mechanical replacement. You can build your own functioning artificial arm using simple materials such as cardboard, plastic straws, and thread.

DIFFICULTY
Tricky

WHAT YOU NEED

Thick thread
(80 in)

Black paint

Ruler

Double-sided tape

Strong tape

2 black bendy plastic straws

3 gold plastic straws

Scissors

Paintbrush

Pencil

Thin gold construction paper (for decoration)

Thick, corrugated cardboard
(10 x 17 in)

Use metal-colored straws to make the arm look more mechanical.

START HERE

1

Paint the corrugated cardboard black. Use the template on pages 122–123 to trace an arm shape on it. Cut out the arm shape and two extra strips that measure 1.5 x 12.5 in and 1.5 x 13.5 in.

IN A GALAXY FAR, FAR AWAY....

Major advances in medical technology have enabled droid surgeons to use cybernetics to replace lost limbs. Whether a limb is destroyed in a lightsaber battle or by a thermal detonator blast, the mechanical replacements offer full and, in many cases, enhanced functionality.

Shorter cardboard strip on the back of the arm for extra support

2

Depending on whether you want to use your right or left hand, chose one side of the cardboard arm as the palm. Flip the arm over and stick the shorter strip onto the back with double-sided tape.

Longer cardboard strip for hand grip

3

This is tricky to do on your own, so ask an adult to help.

Now turn the arm over to the palm side and use strong tape to stick the longer cardboard strip around the arm's widest part to make a hand grip. Leave a gap big enough to fit your own hand through.

4

Use ruler to bend fingers and thumb

Fold

On the palm of your cardboard arm use a ruler to make three folds in each finger and two folds in the thumb. These folds will become the joints of your "mechno-fingers."

BATTLE SCARS

Before he was known as Darth Vader, Anakin lost his right arm fighting Count Dooku. After turning to the dark side and becoming Darth Vader, he lost his left arm and both legs in a battle against Obi-Wan Kenobi. Years later, on Cloud City, Darth Vader is responsible for cutting off Luke Skywalker's hand during a heated duel.

Short bendy straw part

This is tricky to do on your own, so ask an adult for help.

Palm

7

Using a pencil, pierce a hole below the last joint in the thumb. Cut out the folding part of a bendy straw (see inset) and push it through the hole to the back of the cardboard arm.

8

Bendy straw stuck to the back of the arm

Use strong tape to stick the straw down to the back of the arm. Make sure you leave a small part of the straw poking out on the palm of the arm.

5

Cut out nine small (0.5 in) sections from your gold straw. Use thin strips of strong tape to stick down one straw section between each finger joint and another between the thumb joints.

6

Cut out four longer (1 in) gold straw sections and stick them onto the palm of the arm with slightly wider strips of strong tape. Make sure the longer straw sections line up with the smaller straws.

Darth Vader's body has experienced so much injury that when he is not actively healing, he must be fully encased in his armor.

"HE'S MORE MACHINE NOW THAN MAN."
Obi-Wan Kenobi

9

Cut five lengths of thread, each about 16 inches long. Firmly stick the end of the thread to the tips of each finger and the thumb by wrapping a wide strip of strong tape around them.

10

Pass each length of thread through all the straws on the palm of the arm as shown above. Then poke the thumb thread through the small bendy straw part at the bottom of the thumb.

longer bendy straw part

11

Stick two small gold straw sections along the back of the arm from the thumb to the arm grip. Then cut and stick down a longer bendy straw part to the back of the hand grip.

12

On the back of the arm, pull the thumb thread through the small bendy straw. Then pass it through the two small gold straw sections and finally through the long bendy straw part.

HOW IT WORKS

MUSCLES AND TENDONS

The muscles that make your fingers open and close (among other hand movements) are located in your forearms. They are attached to bands of connective tissue called flexor tendons, which form a strong, flexible connection between muscle and bone.

FLEXING MECHNO MUSCLE

When using Anakin's mechno-arm, the flexor tendons on the front and back of your hand allow you to close your fingers and thumb into a fist and then open your hand. As you operate the cybernetic arm, your fingers act like forearm muscles, pulling thread "tendons" to contract the mechno-arm's fingers.

Flexor tendons open and close fingers and thumb

Forearm muscles

More than 30 muscles in the hand and forearm work together in complex ways to achieve a wide range of movement.

WHY NOT TRY?

Humanoid droids also use cybernetic technology to enhance their mechanical limbs. You could make a battle droid's mechno-arm using cardboard, gold or sand-colored paint, gold thread, and gold tape.

You only need to create three loops for your fingers and thumb to operate your battle droid arm.

This is tricky to do on your own, so ask an adult to help.

13

Turn the arm over, palm side up. Tie a knot at the end of all the threads, for your fingers to go through. Make sure each finger can reach the right knot. Add final decorations now if you wish.

Gold construction paper used for decoration

YOU'VE DONE IT!

14

Slip your hand through the cardboard hand grip and your fingers and thumb through the thread loops. Bend your fingers to operate the arm and use it to pick up light objects.

The always obedient B1 battle droids are designed to replicate and improve on humanoid movement and agility. These droids also significantly reduce production costs by replacing living operators of machinery, vehicles, and weapons.

IN OUR GALAXY...

ROBOTIC INNOVATION

It is very difficult for robotics to replicate the complexity of a human hand, but scientists are making amazing progress. Artificial tendons can be made from high-grade polyethylene and attached to artificial hand bones made from metals, composite materials, or plastic using 3D printing. Movement is powered by small, useful electric motors called servos or by pneumatic systems, which use compressed air.

GLIDING SPEEDER

CREATE A BALLOON HOVERCRAFT

Why travel on the ground when you can hover above it? Speeders defy gravity thanks to repulsorlifts, engines, and thrusters. You don't need such advanced components to build your own hovercraft; you can use a balloon, a pop-up water bottle top, and a CD. It only takes a push to send it gliding on a cushion of air, across any smooth surface.

DIFFICULTY
Medium

WHAT YOU NEED

Glue gun

Glue stick

Scissors

CD

Pop-up water bottle top

Paint

Balloon

Cardboard tube

Ruler

Paintbrush

Colored construction paper

OH MY!
Using a glue gun? Make sure you ask an adult for help.

IN A GALAXY FAR, FAR AWAY....

Speeders are the main form of transportation on many planets. Powered by repulsorlifts, which push against a planet's gravitational pull, speeders can hover above almost any surface. The absence of wheels enables speeders to swiftly and easily maneuver over a variety of terrains. This versatility makes speeders ideal transports for farmers, the military, and scavengers like Rey.

START HERE

1
Glue the pop-up water bottle top over the hole in the center of the CD. For the best result, use a glue gun to do this, but take care and ask an adult for help because the glue will be hot!

2
Close the pop-up top firmly so that no air can get through it. Blow up a balloon and secure its mouth over the pop-up top. This will prevent any air escaping from the balloon.

4

To create a sturdy tube support for your speeder, cut a 2.5 inch slit in the side of a cardboard tube with a pair of scissors. Use a ruler to accurately measure the slit.

5

Insert the scissors at the end of the slit you've just made and cut all the way around the tube. You should now have a small cardboard tube cut through on one side. Put it aside for later.

2.5 in

HOW IT WORKS

EQUAL AND OPPOSITE REACTIONS

When you first open the pop-up bottle top on your hovercraft, air rushes out of the balloon in a downward direction. This pushes the balloon up, in the opposite direction, while the CD's weight keeps the balloon from shooting into the air.

HOW IT HOVERS

A cushion of higher air pressure gets trapped under the CD, allowing the hovercraft to stay slightly off the ground and move around freely without friction slowing it down. When the air inside the balloon escapes, gravity pulls the hovercraft back down to Earth.

Balloon

Air

Higher air pressure

CD

Table

6

Now make the sides of your speeder. Use the template on page 122 to create the left and right sides using construction paper. The two sides should be mirror images of each other.

7

Paint your tube support. When it is dry, stick the sides of your speeder on either side of the tube. Don't stick them over the slit in the tube support; leave that unobstructed in the middle.

WHY NOT TRY?

There are many speeders in the *Star Wars* galaxy. You could build Luke Skywalker's X-34 landspeeder, Padmé Amidala's personal Rian-327 airspeeder, or the Gian speeder used by the Royal Guards of Naboo.

X-34 LANDSPEEDER

RIAN-327 AIRSPEEDER

GIAN SPEEDER

IN OUR GALAXY...

HOVERING TO THE RESCUE

Huge hovercrafts were once used to ferry people across the English Channel. Today they're used more often for rescue and recreation. Their unique ability to hover helps hovercrafts reach areas covered with very shallow water or ice, or to cross tidal mudflats, where quicksand or soft mud won't support conventional land vehicles.

8 Once both sides of your speeder are stuck to the tube support, open the tube and wrap it around the bottom of the balloon, resting it on the CD. Take care with the speeder's sides.

9 Set your speeder on a smooth, flat surface. When you're ready, reach inside the tube support and pull up the pop-up top so air starts to escape from the balloon.

"THE AT-AT'S MY HOME, BUT MY SPEEDER'S EVEN MORE IMPORTANT TO MY SURVIVAL."

Rey

10

Give your speeder hovercraft a gentle push and watch it glide along on a cushion of air. Re-inflate the balloon by blowing through the hole in the CD and try it again.

YOU'VE DONE IT!

DESERT TRAVELER

Farmboy Luke Skywalker dreams of being a fighter pilot. However, he has to settle for crossing the desert sands of Tatooine in his battered old X-34 landspeeder. Luke's X-34 can hover a meter off the ground and travel at up to 250 kph (155 mph). This is due to a powerful repulsorlift engine, which is further boosted by three air-cooled thrust turbines.

Rey has custom built her high-velocity speeder from used parts. These have been scavenged from the junkpiles and starship graveyards of her planet Jaaku.

DIFFICULTY
Tricky

BRILLIANT BB UNITS

BUILD A PERFECTLY BALANCED DROID

BB-8 is a brave and loyal droid who will stop at nothing to help the Resistance defeat the First Order. His circular design allows him to roll along most surfaces, while his astromech droid body is equipped with many useful tools. Now you can create your own wobbling BB-8 model, using hamster balls and some marbles.

Metallic pens and permanent marker pens are good to use for intricate decoration.

IN A GALAXY FAR, FAR AWAY....

BB units represent the latest advancements in astromech droid technology. These rolling droids use state-of-the-art, self-correcting gyroscopes to balance their ball-shaped bodies. Powerful magnetic casters keep their heads attached while they roll at impressive speeds in any direction. Their spherical shape, simplicity of movement, and highly sensitive surface sensors allow them to easily maneuver across many types of terrain.

BB-8 is the trusted aide of Resistance pilot Poe Dameron.

Photoreceptor eye made from bottle top.

WHAT YOU NEED

Large hamster ball

Pencil

Paintbrush

Bottle top

Metallic silver pen

Strong tape

Permanent marker pen

Scissors

Weights (large marbles or pebbles)

Small hamster ball (just one half needed)

Pipe cleaners

Disposable plastic bowl

Paint

Old sock

Hamster balls can be bought online.

"HE'S A BB UNIT! ORANGE AND WHITE: ONE OF A KIND."
Poe Dameron

START HERE

1

Paint the outside of the large hamster ball white for BB-8's body. Do the same with half of the small hamster ball and the outside of the plastic bowl. (These will make BB-8's head.)

2

Use the lid as a guide to paint two orange rings—one at the top and one at the bottom of the large hamster ball. If needed, use a round object, such as a bowl, to create neat circles.

BB-8 rolls at high speed to avoid capture by the First Order on the planet Jakku.

5

Bottle top

Now let's decorate BB-8's head. Add orange and silver details to the small hamster ball half. Paint a bottle top black and stick it on to create BB-8's photoreceptor eye.

3

Trace around a smaller bowl to draw four more rings around the sides of the ball. Use the ball's breathing holes as a guide to help space the rings evenly. Paint the rings orange.

4

Add mechanical details to the large hamster ball using a silver pen and a black permanent marker pen. Look at pictures of droids and machines to decide what you want to add.

A TOOL FOR EACH TASK

The circular panels on BB units are tool-bay disks, which can house all manner of useful gadgets, such as arc welders, magnetic-tipped bolt spinners, and computer interface arms. Owners of BB units are able to change these disks when they want, selecting the best tools for different missions.

Cutting and piercing the bowl can be tricky, so ask an adult to help.

6

Carefully cut the top and rim off the small plastic bowl. This will be placed inside the BB-8 head piece, so make sure the cut edge fits neatly inside the small hamster ball half.

⚠️

7

Pierce a hole in the middle of the bowl using scissors. Twist two pipe cleaners together and poke them through the hole. Secure them to the inside of the bowl with strong tape.

⚠️

8 Place the plastic bowl into BB-8's head piece as shown. Make sure the pipe cleaners are sticking out. Use strong tape to secure the bowl to the inside of the hamster ball.

9 Take the lid off the large hamster ball. Push the pipe cleaners through one of the breathing holes and twist them up against the inside of the hamster ball so they can't fall out.

HOW IT WORKS

CENTER OF GRAVITY

Every object has a center of gravity—a single point on which the force of gravity acts. An object is most stable when its center of gravity is at the lowest possible position.

BALANCING YOUR BB-8 MODEL

Before you add weight to the hamster ball, its center of gravity is at the mid-point of the sphere, so it rolls freely. When you tape marbles to the bottom, their weight shifts the ball's center of gravity downward. If you rock the ball, gravity acts on the raised center of gravity, pulling the marbles back down. This keeps your BB unit upright.

Ball with
no marbles

Ball with
marbles in
stable position

Movement of
ball back to
stable position

KEY ★ = Center of gravity

↓ = Gravity

⬮ = Marbles

10

Put marbles or pebbles into an old sock and tie it tightly. Use strong tape to secure the weighted sock inside the hamster ball, opposite BB-8's head. Close the lid and gently rock your BB-8!

YOU'VE DONE IT!

BB-9E's flat-shaped head can be re-created using a disposable black plastic bowl with the rim cut off.

WHY NOT TRY?

BB-8 is friendly, but Imperial droid BB-9E is not! Build your own BB baddie using black and silver, and decorate it with open grilles instead of tool panels.

IN OUR GALAXY...

ROCK THE BOAT

If you've ever climbed into a boat, you'll have felt it wobble until you lower its center of gravity by sitting down. Large ships are stabilized using ballast—heavy material, such as water, stored at the bottom of the boat.

DON'T ROCK THE BOAT

The *Vasa*, a famous Swedish warship, was tipped over by a gust of wind on her maiden voyage in 1628. The big boat had been designed with its center of gravity too high, so it couldn't resist the force of the wind.

DIFFICULTY
Easy

INVISIBLE FORCE

USE THE FORCE OF STATIC ELECTRICITY

The Force is a mystical energy field that flows through everything in the galaxy. Rare individuals have the ability to channel and even master the Force, using it to control objects—and sometimes even people. You can unlock your own abilities using science... Create a lightsaber and use it to suspend and move a tinsel orb in the air!

Your lightsaber will be able to control the movement of the tinsel in the air.

IN A GALAXY FAR, FAR AWAY....

The Jedi are Force users and they require much training in the ways of the Force. They must learn how to channel the Force when they need it, and to control its incredible power. Luke Skywalker uses training remotes to hone his lightsaber skills. These tiny, round droids hover in the air and fire sting beams. A Jedi must use the Force to anticipate the next shot and deflect it with their lightsaber.

WHAT YOU NEED

Thin mylar tinsel
strands (roughly
12 in long)

Construction paper

Double-sided
tape

Black tape

Gold tape

Scissors

PVC rod (roughly 25 in long, 1 in wide)

You need "mylar tinsel" for this project,
which can be bought online.

Keeping the
tinsel orb in the
air takes a few
tries. But practice
makes perfect.

Decorate your
lightsaber to match
the lightsaber of
your favorite Jedi.

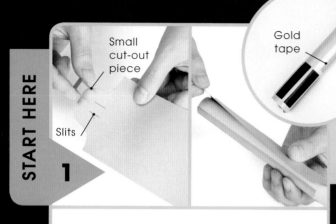

Small cut-out piece

Slits

Gold tape

1

Using the template on page 124, make a lightsaber handle from construction paper. Poke the small cut-out piece through slits in the large sheet. Tape the handle to the PVC rod and decorate it.

2

Carefully lay out several strands of mylar tinsel together and tie a knot at either end, approximately 6 in apart. Trim off any excess tinsel at the ends.

HOW IT WORKS

CHARGING...

When you rub a plastic rod on your hair, negatively charged particles called electrons move between your hair and the rod. This results in the build up of an electrical charge on the plastic rod called static electricity.

FORCE OF REPULSION

When you drop the tinsel on the charged plastic rod, electrons jump between the rod and the tinsel, giving each strand the same static charge as the rod. Objects with similar charges push each other away, so the tinsel strands repel each other and the rod repels the tinsel, making it float.

Mylar tinsel

PVC lightsaber

Electrical repulsion

Jedi use the Force in many ways, always with good intentions. Jedi Master Yoda uses the Force to stop falling rocks and stone columns from crushing him.

3

Rub the PVC rod against your hair or woollen clothing to charge it up with static electricity. You might have to rub it for a minute or two to build up enough of a charge.

4

Drop the tinsel onto the PVC rod. If the rod is sufficiently charged, the tinsel will "pop" open and float. This part may take a few attempts to get right, but don't give up, young Jedi!

YOU'VE DONE IT!

"THE FORCE IS... AN ENERGY FIELD CREATED BY ALL LIVING THINGS."
Obi-Wan Kenobi to
Luke Skywalker

IN OUR GALAXY...

SAFER SMOKE

Static electricity is used to remove dust and other unwanted particles from factory emissions. Factory smoke travels up through a chimney, which is lined with charged metal plates. The plates set up an invisible electric field that attracts pollutant particles. Similar technology is used in some home air purifiers.

DIFFICULTY
Tricky

SPEEDY PODRACERS

BUILD YOUR OWN RACING MACHINE

Podracing is one of the most dangerous sports in the galaxy. It's fast, furious, and unpredictable. Podracing involves heavily modified vehicles, untrained pilots, and huge bursts of energy—all of which make it a very popular sport. You too can build a podracer that speeds along on a burst of energy. Luckily, it's not nearly as dangerous!

Turbines painted onto cardboard disks.

WHAT YOU NEED

3 ice-pop sticks

Straw

Paintbrush

Strong glue

Thread

2 wooden skewers

4 milk bottle caps

Adhesive putty

PVA glue

Scissors

Metallic pens (gold and silver)

Elastic band

Electrical tape

Thick cardboard sheet

Paint

Wire

2 cardboard tubes

Pointed wing-tips are dangerous for racing rivals.

Cardboard pilot sits in the pod's cockpit.

Engine paneling drawn on with metallic marker pen.

IN A GALAXY FAR, FAR AWAY....

Crowds turn out by the thousands to watch one of the galaxy's most thrilling and dangerous events: podracing! Each podracer typically features two powerful engines and a one-man cockpit and can reach speeds of 947 kph (588 mph). Some pilots are responsible for designing and building their own podracers.

START HERE

1

Take three ice-pop sticks. Carefully cut or snap one of them in half and glue it to the other two, so it connects them near one end. This will become the front of your podracer.

2

Cut a plastic straw into one long piece and two short ones. Stick the long piece to the front end, parallel to the cross stick. Stick the short pieces to the opposite ends.

"I'M BUILDING A PODRACER."
Anakin Skywalker

Piercing a hole in the bottle caps is tricky, so ask an adult for help.

Engine support

5

Carefully pierce a hole in each bottle cap. Slide the caps onto the front and back skewers, gluing them if required. Cover the sides of the back two caps with electrical tape to add traction.

6

Trace the engine support template on page 123 onto cardboard. Then cut, fold, and glue the engine support to the front end of your podracer. The cardboard must not touch the wheels.

3

Flip the podracer over. Carefully cut a skewer in half and push one half through the straw at the front and the other half through the two small straw pieces at the back.

Podracing rivals Anakin Skywalker and Sebulba go head to head at the Boonta Eve Classic race on Tatooine.

4

Cut two small skewer pieces. Attach one to the ice-pop stick at the front with strong glue. Use thread to tightly attach the other small piece to the skewer at the back of the podracer.

Ask an adult to apply strong glue for you.

Attaching the wire to the tubes is tricky, so ask an adult for help.

7

Using the template on page 123, cut the pod support out of cardboard. Fold it as shown and stick the two "feet" onto the ice-pop stick ends at the back of the podracer.

8

Attach wire between two cardboard tubes and glue them onto the engine support at the front of the podracer. The wire should be tight enough so it stops the tubes from sagging outward.

9

Pod base

Cockpit parts

Pilot

Finished cockpit

Cut the cockpit parts and pilot out of cardboard using templates on pages 122–123. Assemble as shown, attaching the parts with PVA glue. Stick the finished cockpit to the pod support.

10

Stick two cardboard strips between the tubes and the pod. You may need to add some putty to weigh down the back of the podracer. Stick some on the ice-pop sticks near the rear axle.

HOW IT WORKS

STORED ENERGY

Energy is needed to make a machine move. It can be stored in different ways. Many machines today rely on energy stored in electric batteries or in chemical fuels such as gasoline.

PODRACER POWER

To power your podracer, elastic potential energy is stored in the wound-up elastic band. As you wind it, the energy builds up. When you let go, the energy that is released by the elastic band returning to its original shape turns the podracer's axle, spinning the wheels.

As the band unwinds, it turns the axle and wheels

Rear axle

Stored elastic energy is released when you let go

Ben Quadinaros's podracer

Ebe E. Endocott's podracer

Gasgano's podracer

Clegg Holdfast's podracer

11 ▷

Decorate your podracer using paint, metallic pens, and extra pieces of cardboard. You could create fins or spoilers for your podracer. What else can you think of?

12 ▷

Loop an elastic band around the small skewer piece at the front and the one at the back. Twist the rear skewer piece round and round, winding up the band. Then let go.

YOU'VE DONE IT!

WHY NOT TRY?

Podracers are as unique as their pilots. Any shape or color is fine—as long as they fly fast. What about building one of these?

Dusty, rusty colors show that the podracer has been well used.

Engine sparks can be created with a pipe cleaner, too!

IN OUR GALAXY...

WIND-UP MOTION

Wind-up toys use stored energy to move. When you turn the crank or key, you tighten the small metal coil inside the toy, which stores up elastic energy. When you release the crank, the spring unwinds and the energy is transformed into kinetic energy—the energy of motion.

DIFFICULTY
Medium

EWOK CATAPULT

BUILD AN AMAZING LAUNCHER

The Ewoks of Endor are small, but they play a huge role in the battle against the Empire. Their fearsome, handmade weapons are made from logs and sticks, yet they can destroy some of the toughest Imperial war machines. Try building your own catapult from the same sort of materials the Ewoks use—just collect some sticks!

WHAT YOU NEED

Scissors

Sturdy sticks (5 medium sticks, 4 longer sticks, 3 shorter sticks, 2 sticks that bend at the end or 1 thick stick that forks at the end, plus spare sticks)

Twine

Elastic bands

Scrunched-up paper balls

START HERE

Extra support

1

Use twine to firmly tie four sturdy sticks together in a square, creating a base. Make sure the sticks overlap at the corners. Attach a fifth stick diagonally for extra support.

IN A GALAXY FAR, FAR AWAY....

The primitive Ewoks of the Moon of Endor use logs and branches to build catapults. They can hurl stones and boulders much farther than anyone can throw by hand. Invaders of Endor, beware!

An extra pair of hands will be useful for this step. Ask someone to help.

Sling

2

Choose four longer sticks and tie one to each corner of the base with twine. Slip a thick elastic band around the front two sticks, just under halfway down. This will become the sling.

3

Use twine to join the upright sticks at the top to form two parallel triangles. The elastic-band sling connects the two triangles, and it may slightly pull them toward each other. This is fine.

4 Additional support (if needed)

Triangle supports

Lay a shorter stick across the top of the triangle supports and tie it on. Attach a similar sized stick halfway down (just above the rubber band), and a third stick near the bottom.

5 Cradle

Catapult arm made from two sticks

Take the two sticks that fork at one end and tie them together to make the catapult arm. Wrap twine loosely around the forks to create a cradle for the ammunition.

HOW IT WORKS

EVERLASTING ENERGY

Energy isn't created or destroyed. It is transformed from one form to another. A catapult can demonstrate energy transformations in action.

CHEMICAL, ELASTIC, KINETIC

When you pull the catapult arm back, the chemical energy in your muscles—from the food you eat—becomes elastic potential energy, now stored in the elastic-band sling. Then, when you let go, the elastic energy becomes kinetic energy —the energy of motion—launching your ammunition through the air.

Kinetic energy (energy of motion)

Elastic band (elastic energy)

Tying the elastic band around the beam is tricky. Ask an adult for help.

Only fire light objects from your catapult and *never* aim at a person or animal!

6

Attach the arm to the middle beam of the frame with an elastic band. Loop and tie the band around the beam and arm until it is secured. The cradle should rest behind the top beam.

7

Make sure the elastic-band sling rests on top of the catapult arm. Place your scrunched-up paper balls on the cradle, gently pull the arm down, and release!

YOU'VE DONE IT!

To fire a catapult, a single Ewok simply pulls and releases the trigger rope, sending the rocks flying!

IN OUR GALAXY...

ELASTIC ENERGY

Elastic slingshots haven't been used on our planet for all that long. These small projectile weapons use a new, improved form of synthetic rubber called vulcanized rubber, which was discovered in 1839. The stretchy handheld shooters have been used for everything from mischief-making to hunting, but are rarely used in combat.

R2-D2 HOLOPROJECTOR

MAKE A CELL PHONE BOX PROJECTOR

Need to send a message across the galaxy? Just switch on a holoprojector! These gadgets use light to create three-dimensional (3D) holograms. You can build your own projector and use light to display 2D images. All you need is a cell phone, cardboard boxes, a magnifying glass, and a few household items to project your own images... just like R2-D2!

The light from the cell phone passes through a magnifying glass lens placed over a hole in the front of the box.

WHAT YOU NEED

Cardboard box (8.5 x 6 x 4 in)   Magnifying glass   Pencil   Black duct tape or masking tape   Scissors

Cardboard box (6 x 4 x 4 in)   Paintbrush   Newspaper   Measuring cup   PVA glue   2 large bowls   Paint   Ruler   Adhesive putty

Cell phone   Elastic band   Lightweight cardboard sheets   Plastic wrap

IN A GALAXY FAR, FAR AWAY....

Holoprojectors create 3D images by manipulating beams of light. They can display static images, recorded messages, and live audio-visual feeds. Due to the large amount of power they use, most holoprojectors display a blue-and-white image. They come in various sizes, from astromech-mounted units to simple handheld devices.

The picture on the cell phone is projected onto a wall or a screen.

1 Securely tape the bottom of the large box, leaving the top open. On one of the small sides of the box trace around the magnifying glass lens with a pencil. Draw a smaller circle within this circle.

2 Use scissors to cut out the inner circle, then set aside the cardboard disk. On the inside of the box, stick the lens against the hole with strong tape. Make sure you tape over any gaps.

Cutting out the lens hole is tricky, so ask an adult for help.

5 Once the papier-mâché dome is dry, paint it gray. Then use the cardboard disk you set aside to trace a circle on the top of the dome. Cut out the circle to make a lens hole.

6 Use strong tape to fully seal the small box. Paint both boxes black, including the inside of the larger box's flaps. You may need two coats of paint to make the boxes very black.

3

Next, use scissors to cut two slits in the top flaps of the box about ²/₃ of the way down from the lens and fold them out. Then seal together the longer flaps with strong tape.

4

Create R2-D2's dome. Place plastic wrap around the outside of a bowl that is a bit larger than the small side of the box. Papier-mâché the bowl in the same way as the Death Star (see pages 16–17).

R2-D2 accesses a holomap providing a full blueprint of General Grievous's command ship, the *Invisible Hand*.

"HELP ME OBI-WAN KENOBI. YOU'RE MY ONLY HOPE."
Princess Leia

7

Tape the larger lens box to the small box so that it overhangs a little. Then securely tape the dome to the front of the lens box, making sure the hole lines up with the lens.

8

Cut out two large triangles of lightweight cardboard. Wrap them around both sides of the dome and both boxes. Secure the triangles firmly to the dome with strong tape.

9

Cut out and tape a large rectangular strip of cardboard around the bottom of the dome so it hides the boxes. Cover any gaps at the front of your model with small cardboard triangles.

10

Once all the pieces of cardboard have been securely taped in place, paint your model to look like R2-D2's head. Use the photo above as a guide to the astromech's design.

HOW IT WORKS

LIGHT BENDERS

A lens is a piece of transparent material that is used for forming an image by focusing light. Lenses are used in magnifying glasses, microscopes, and telescopes. They can bend light rays and refocus them to enable us to see things too small for the naked eye, or view faraway objects such as planets.

PROJECTING IMAGES

Projectors use a convex lens, which bulges out in the center. When light rays pass through it they are bent inward and meet at a spot known as the focal point. Past the focal point a projected image is flipped upside down and enlarged when it makes contact with a screen or wall.

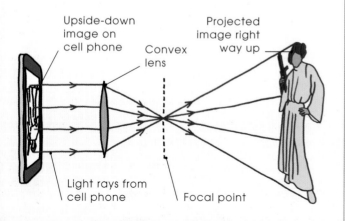

Upside-down image on cell phone

Projected image right way up

Convex lens

Light rays from cell phone

Focal point

Rebel Alliance leaders discuss strategy around a holoprojection of the Death Star, a planet-destroying battle station built by the Galactic Empire.

Put your phone on its brightest setting.

11

Save a *Star Wars* image to your phone. Turn off auto screen rotation and flip the image landscape. Put the phone into the box sideways, with the image upside down. Secure it with adhesive putty.

12

Close the flaps with an elastic band to keep out light. Point the projector at a plain wall. Turn out the lights and focus your picture by moving the projector closer to or farther away from the wall.

YOU'VE DONE IT!

IN OUR GALAXY...

THE BIGGER PICTURE

When you go to the movies, small images on a reel of film, or digital images, are projected through a powerful lens that magnifies them onto the big screen. Many images are displayed every second one after the other, to give the illusion of moving scenes.

DIFFICULTY
Easy

DEATH STAR SUPERLASER

POP A BALLOON WITH PURE ENERGY

The Death Star destroys planets by channeling its immensely powerful energy through kyber crystals and focusing the laser beams onto a planet. You can harness the sun's energy in much the same way, using a lens to focus sunlight and create intense heat. All you need is a sunny day, a magnifying glass, and a balloon.

IN A GALAXY FAR, FAR AWAY....

The Death Star is a massive battle station—the size of a moon and home to more than 1 million crew. What makes it unique is its superlaser, a weapon unlike any other. Created by brilliant scientist Galen Erso, the superlaser focuses energy through kyber crystals into a beam of terrifying power. Erso understands the danger of this weapon, so he secretly builds a flaw into the design, allowing the rebels to destroy it.

WHAT YOU NEED

Funnel Balloon Sunglasses

Flour Glitter Magnifying glass Permanent marker pen

A beach-covered planet would explode in a cloud of blue and gold.

START HERE

1

Using the funnel, carefully pour a small amount of flour and glitter into the balloon. Different colored balloons or glitter will produce different effects.

2

Blow up the balloon until it's almos at bursting point—remember to ta a deep breath first! Then firmly tie the end of the balloon in a single knot to prevent any air escaping.

3 Use a permanent marker pen to draw a rebel symbol onto the balloon as best as you can. This will indicate where the rebel base is located on your big balloon planet.

4 On a sunny day, stand with your back to the sun. Hold the magnifying glass up and focus the sun's light directly onto the rebel symbol. You should see a bright circle on the balloon.

HOW IT WORKS

LIGHT BENDER

Magnifying glass lenses have a special convex shape that bulges outward. The curved glass bends the light rays as they pass through it, making the rays meet at one spot on the other side, called a focal point.

EARTH'S STAR

Light rays from the sun carry lots of energy. A small lens like a magnifying glass can concentrate the sun's energy on an object at a focal point. This creates enough heat to pop a balloon. Larger lenses can focus even more heat and energy.

The Death Star generates eight primary energy beams focused through thousands of kyber crystals. These are concentrated into a single superlaser. At full power, the beam can destroy an entire planet.

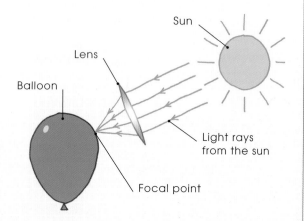

Sun

Lens

Balloon

Light rays from the sun

Focal point

OH MY!

Never look directly at the sun! Make sure you wear sunglasses to protect your eyes from bright sunlight.

5 Move the magnifying glass toward or away from the balloon until you've focused the sunlight into the smallest possible circle over your rebel target. Your Death Star beam is powering up...

6 Hold the light beam steady on the same spot until the heat created by the beam pops the balloon. You have destroyed the rebel base—along with your entire balloon world!

YOU'VE DONE IT!

IN OUR GALAXY...

SOLAR POWER

Humans have used sunlight-focusing lenses to light fires for more than 2,000 years. Today, lenses are used in some solar panels, to focus sunlight onto photovoltaic cells. These cells contain special semiconducting materials that turn the sun's energy into electricity.

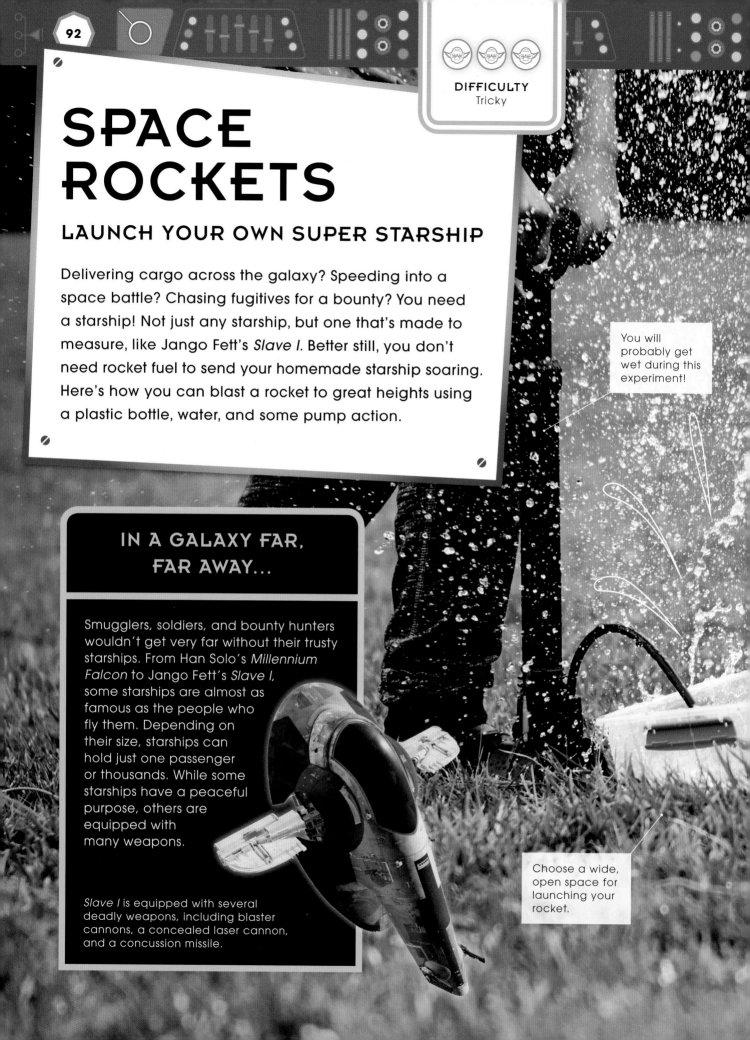

DIFFICULTY
Tricky

SPACE ROCKETS

LAUNCH YOUR OWN SUPER STARSHIP

Delivering cargo across the galaxy? Speeding into a space battle? Chasing fugitives for a bounty? You need a starship! Not just any starship, but one that's made to measure, like Jango Fett's *Slave I*. Better still, you don't need rocket fuel to send your homemade starship soaring. Here's how you can blast a rocket to great heights using a plastic bottle, water, and some pump action.

You will probably get wet during this experiment!

IN A GALAXY FAR, FAR AWAY...

Smugglers, soldiers, and bounty hunters wouldn't get very far without their trusty starships. From Han Solo's *Millennium Falcon* to Jango Fett's *Slave I*, some starships are almost as famous as the people who fly them. Depending on their size, starships can hold just one passenger or thousands. While some starships have a peaceful purpose, others are equipped with many weapons.

Slave I is equipped with several deadly weapons, including blaster cannons, a concealed laser cannon, and a concussion missile.

Choose a wide, open space for launching your rocket.

WHAT YOU NEED

Bike or ball pump

Jug of water

Funnel

1 liter plastic bottle

Large plastic container

Wine cork (cut in half)

Double-sided tape

Scissors

Paintbrush

Ball pump needle

Colored construction paper

Permanent marker pen

Paint

START HERE

1

Bottle holder

Using the template on page 125, cut the bottle holder out of construction paper. Fold it into a tube as shown and tape the edges firmly together using double-sided tape.

2

Slave I base

Decorate bottle holder to look like your favorite *Star Wars* ship. The templates on pages 124–125 have some shapes to create *Slave I*. Add your own details with paint or permanent marker pens.

3

Once you have added all your decorations, such as wings, weapons, and *Star Wars* symbols, place the big plastic bottle into the bottle holder. Secure it firmly with double-sided tape.

Slave I wing

4

Your starship is now complete! Use the funnel to pour water into the bottle. You only want to fill it up about ⅓ of the way, leaving plenty of space inside to pump full of air.

HOW IT WORKS

USE THE FORCE (OF THRUST)

Launching a rocket into space requires many calculations about the rocket's weight and shape, air resistance, and, most importantly, thrust. Thrust is the force that gets rockets off the ground.

PUMPED PRESSURE

While real rockets use rocket fuel for thrust, water rockets use water. As air is pumped into the bottle, the pressure inside increases. When the pressure gets high enough, the bottle releases it by pushing out the water and cork, propelling the bottle upwards.

Upward motion

Increasing air pressure

Released air pressure

Air pumped into bottle

Cork

Expelled water

WHY NOT TRY?
You could make rockets look like different *Star Wars* ships, such as an Imperial shuttle. The shuttle transports important officers of the Empire across the galaxy, and has three wings: one fixed at the top and two folding ones on the sides.

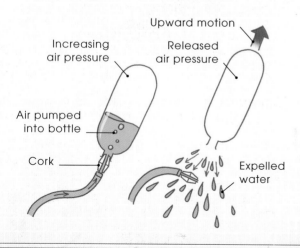

Try making wings that fold up and down for an Imperial shuttle.

Cutting the cork and pushing the needle through it is tricky, so ask an adult for help.

5

Push the ball pump needle through the (half) cork until it pokes out the other side. Connect the needle to the pump and twist it in tightly to stop any air from escaping.

6

Insert the cork into the bottle and make sure it is secured very tightly. You could push the cork into the bottle with a twisting motion to make sure it's as tight as it can be.

DELTA-7 INTERCEPTOR

Obi-Wan's sleek, arrow-shaped starfighter is built for speed. It also has a little socket for an astromech droid.

TIE FIGHTER

TIE fighters are small yet scary ships, with a round cockpit and big, angular wings. They are little and light, which makes them super fast.

RZ-1 A-WING

A-wings are swift starfighters used by the Rebel Alliance to dart into battle. Their wedge shape helps them fly at

IN OUR GALAXY...

RACING INTO SPACE

Humans use rocket science to launch many things—from satellites to astronauts and space stations—out of Earth's atmosphere and into space. Rocket technology allows us to go where no humans or machines have gone before, to explore our Solar System and learn more about galaxies far, far away.

7

Set up your launch pad in a large, open area. Place the bottle, cork-side down, in the plastic container, so that the bottom of the bottle is pointing upward, but away from you.

8

Make sure everyone is standing behind the pump (and is prepared to get wet!). Check nobody is close enough to be in the bottle's path. Begin your countdown... 5, 4, 3...

"I CAN ASSURE YOU THEY WILL NEVER GET ME ONTO ONE OF THOSE DREADFUL STARSHIPS."

C-3PO

9

YOU'VE DONE IT!

Pump air into the bottle. It will get harder to pump as the bottle fills with air. Eventually the air pressure forces the cork and water out, launching the rocket into the air. You have lift off!

Jango Fett's *Slave I* chases Obi-Wan Kenobi's Delta-7 interceptor through an asteroid field. Both ships are built for speed, but while *Slave I* is built for attack, the interceptor is designed for maneuverability.

DIFFICULTY
Easy

GLOBE OF PEACE

MAKE A GLOWING ICY ORB

When the Naboo and the Gungans unite to defeat a common threat, they celebrate peace, unity, and friendship by exchanging the Globe of Peace. Legend says that this artifact of the Naboo people glows with plasma energy harvested from the locap plant found in the deep seas. Here is how you can create your own Globe of Peace.

This globe is a temporary treasure—the ice will melt after a while.

Put lots of glow sticks inside the globe for a more spectacular result.

IN A GALAXY FAR, FAR AWAY....

Though they share a planet, the land-dwelling Naboo and the underwater Gungans do not always see eye to eye. When the greedy Trade Federation attempts to take over their peaceful world, it forces these neighbors to put their past behind them and work together to defeat the invading droid army. They celebrate their victory with a great parade and ceremony, establishing decades of peace between the two species.

WHAT YOU NEED

Ruler

Spoon

Scissors

Balloon   Glow sticks

You will also need water and a freezer.

START HERE

You may need to create space in the freezer for the balloon.

1

Place the mouth of a balloon around your tap. Fill the balloon with cold water until it is around 5 inches wide. This can be tricky, so ask an adult for help. Once full, tie the end.

2

Put the balloon in the freezer, making sure it isn't squashed so it stays round. Remove it after around 9 hours, when it feels solid. Don't leave it too long—the middle should still be liquid.

5

Put glow sticks inside the globe and set it on a plate. Turn out the lights to see your Globe of Peace in all its shining glory.

YOU'VE DONE IT!

4

⚠️ Ask an adult to break a hole in the ice and pour the water out. The ice should be thinnest at the bottom of the globe, where it was resting in the freezer, so break through there.

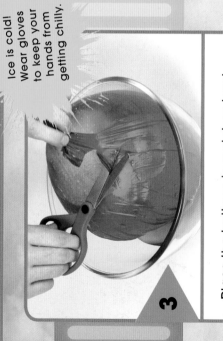

3

Ice is cold! Wear gloves to keep your hands from getting chilly.

Place the balloon in a sink or bowl and carefully cut away the rubber. The water inside the balloon should have frozen into an icy sphere and the middle should still be liquid.

IN OUR GALAXY...

FROZEN WORLD

During winter in cold parts of the world, lakes freeze into sheets of ice. However, it is the top layer of water that transforms into solid, glasslike ice. This ice layer helps to insulate the water below, keeping it in a liquid state. Fish and other wildlife can survive in this watery world beneath the icy crust.

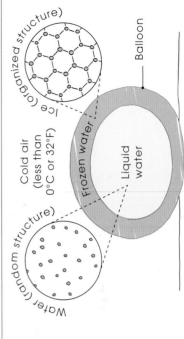

Gungan leader Boss Nass holds up the beautiful Globe of Peace for the citizens of Naboo to admire.

HOW IT WORKS

CHILLING OUT

When water molecules are in their liquid state they have a lot of energy to bounce around. If the molecules are cooled, they lose energy and slow down. When the temperature drops to freezing point (0°C/32°F), the molecules snap into an organized pattern and become solid ice.

OUTSIDE IN

The water inside the balloon freezes in stages as it cools down. The water nearest the outside of the balloon freezes first, creating a shell of ice with a liquid center. If left in the cold, the globe will eventually freeze completely—from the outside in!

Ice (organized structure)

Water (random structure)

Cold air (less than 0°C or 32°F)

Frozen water

Liquid water

Balloon

INTERSTELLAR INSTRUMENTS

FORM YOUR OWN MUSICAL BAND

Whether you're into the swinging sounds of the Modal Nodes or the jaunty beats of Shag Kava, these talented bands have wowed audiences from Mos Eisley's Cantina to Maz Kanata's castle. You can lead your own three-piece ensemble, but first you need to make a trio of musical instruments inspired by the galaxy's favorite performers.

The elastic band guitar's elaborate decoration takes its cue from the Shag Kava's seven-string hallikset.

The balloon drum's natural stylings are inspired by the Ewoks' makeshift village drums.

KLOO HORN

"Fiery" Figrin D'an is the leader of the Bith band, the Modal Nodes, who perform regularly at Mos Eisley Cantina. D'an is a master of the kloo horn, a double-reeded wind instrument that is popular throughout the galaxy.

IN A GALAXY FAR, FAR AWAY....

Shag Kava boasts four of the galaxy's finest musicians. Sudswater Dillifay Glon takes the lead on the seven-string hallikset, with Infrablue Zedbeddy Coggins on the hypolliope horn cluster, Ubert "Sticks" Quaril on the xyloxan, and Taybin Ralorsa providing the smooth vocals. This traveling band regular appears at pirate Maz Kanata's castle on the planet Takodana.

The bottle flute's design is based on a blend of the kloo horn and bandfill instruments played by the Modal Nodes.

ELASTIC BAND GUITAR

START HERE

1

Stretch a few elastic bands of different thicknesses around a plastic food container. The thicker the elastic band the deeper the sound it makes when it's strummed.

WHAT YOU NEED

Plastic food container

Strong tape

Elastic bands

Corrugated cardboard

Paint

Scissors

Paintbrush

Twine

Permanent marker pen

4

Mold the long cardboard strips around the base of the guitar to form its walls, taping strips together as needed. Then tape the tabs to the base to secure the walls in place.

Head

Fret

Bridge parts

7

Now you're ready to start decorating. First, cut out additional cardboard pieces for the bridge, fret, and head of the guitar and tape them down. Then cut up several lengths of twine.

2

For the base and top of the guitar, cut out two cardboard circles that are wider than the plastic container and two cardboard rectangles. Tape each rectangle to one of the circles.

3

Tabs

Cut out several long cardboard strips. Then cut and fold tabs along both edges of the strips. Make sure the width of the strips (excluding tabs) is greater than the height of the container.

5

Once the walls have been made, put the plastic container inside the guitar body. To stop the container moving around, attach it to the base of the guitar with double-sided tape.

6

In the top of the guitar you made in step 2, cut a small circle to create a hole for you to strum the elastic bands. Tape this last big piece onto the rest of the guitar body.

8

Head

Fret

Bridge

Attach the twine from the bridge to the fret and head of the guitar, and cut off any excess. Then apply paint and use permanent marker pens for fine details. Use the design above as inspiration.

9

YOU'
DONE

When the paint has dried you can make music by strumming or plucking the elastic bands. Remember, don't pluck the twine as these are only used for decoration.

BOTTLE FLUTE

WHAT YOU NEED

Small plastic bottle

2 straws

Scissors

Balloon

Corrugated cardboard

Elastic band

Strong tape

Paint

Permanent
marker pen

Paintbrush

START HERE

1

Ask an adult to pierce a hole in the bottom of the bottle and in the side, big enough to fit a straw. Cut into a balloon and stretch a bit of it over the top of the bottle. Secure with an elastic band.

4

Roll up a rectangular piece of corrugated cardboard to create a handle and secure it with tape. Attach one end of the handle to the bottle with strong tape.

7

Use the star tabs to tape the three cones to the sides of the bottle. For a round bottle, keep the cones evenly spaced. Add other decorations, such as a cardboard circle.

2

A shorter straw produces higher notes.

Discard ⅓ of a straw and then cut a few evenly spaced holes in the straw at one end. Push the other end of the straw through the hole in the bottom of the bottle almost to the lid.

3

Now push the other straw through the hole on the side of the bottle until it nearly touches the other side. Leave a little space between the end of the longer straw and the side of the bottle.

5

Now decorate your flute. Cut out a circle of cardboard and draw a star shape in the center. Then use scissors to cut a slit from the edge of the circle to the star and cut out the star.

6

Fold back the star tabs and mold the cardboard circle into a cone shape. Use double-sided tape to secure the cone. Make three of these cones for your bottle flute.

8

Finish decorating by painting and drawing on your bottle flute, including the cones, the handle, and even the straws. Make sure you leave space on the longer straw to blow through.

9

Take a deep breath and play your flute by blowing through the longer straw. Try creating different sounds by covering the holes in the small straw with your thumb.

YOU'VE DONE IT!

BALLOON DRUM

START HERE

1

Cut into a balloon and stretch a piece of it over the top of a cardboard container. Make sure the balloon is tautly stretched before you secure it in place with an elastic band.

Properly dispose of the rest of the balloon!

4

After the paint has dried, push split pins into the cardboard strips—five at the top, five at the bottom. The split pins at either end must line up so you can criss-cross twine between them.

WHAT YOU NEED

Cardboard container

Corrugated cardboard sheet

Paintbrush

Gold balloon

Elastic band

Strong tape

Split pins

Twine

Paint

Scissors

HOW IT WORKS

SOUND WAVES

When an object vibrates in the air, it compresses air molecules to create pressure waves. Repeating vibrations in the air are called sound waves.

We can detect sound waves when they enter the ear canal and make our eardrums vibrate. The vibrations are passed on to an organ, the cochlea, which translates vibrations into electrical signals that travel to the brain along auditory nerves. This is how we hear.

2

Wrap a rectangular piece of cardboard around the container and attach it with strong tape. Then cut out, wrap, and tape two thin cardboard strips to the top and bottom of the container.

3

Paint your balloon drum. Apply a dark base coat and add layers of different colored paint to create any pattern you like. It could be a camouflage design or something more vibrant.

5

Once you've finished, play your balloon drum. You can either use your hands or light objects to beat the top of the drum. Take care not to puncture the balloon!

YOU'VE DONE IT!

IN OUR GALAXY...

GOOD VIBRATIONS

Some of the sound waves from percussion, wind, and string instruments keep vibrating inside the instrument's body. An instrument's shape, size, and construction materials give it a unique wave signature. That's why drums, flutes, and guitars sound so different.

SYNTHESIZING SOUNDS

Like the human ear, synthesizers turn sounds into electrical signals. This allows musicians to manipulate individual sound waves. It also makes it possible to imitate wave signatures from any musical instrument, or make sounds that can't be produced in nature.

Air molecules

Compressed air molecules

Drum beat vibrations create sound waves

Ear drum

Cochlea

Auditory nerve

SUPER SPEEDER BIKE

MAKE A HIGH-FLYING HOOP GLIDER

Zoom into action with your very own speeder bike! As fast as they are dangerous, speeder bikes are small enough to go where other vehicles can't. With these "hoop gliders," you can re-create the thrilling flight of a speeder bike using straws and paper.

"KEEP ON THAT ONE! I'LL TAKE THESE TWO!"

Luke Skywalker to Princess Leia as they chase scout troopers on speeder bikes

IN A GALAXY FAR, FAR AWAY....

Speeder bikes are used for scouting and escort missions. During the Clone Wars, Biker Advanced Recon Commando (BARC) speeders are piloted by specially trained clone troopers. Flying a few feet off the ground, the BARC speeder can reach speeds of more than 500 kph (310 mph).

The Empire uses modified speeder bikes. Stripped down to the bare essentials, the 74-Z speeder is lighter, which allows its pilot to reach even greater speeds.

Sponge on paint to create a rusted look for your speeder bike.

Draw extra details with a metallic pen.

WHAT YOU NEED

Double-sided tape (regular tape will work, too)

Glue stick

Paperclips

Scissors

2 plastic straws

Paint

Construction paper

1 Use the template on page 120 to cut out the shapes for your hoop glider from construction paper. You could decorate your glider with paint, marker pens, or colored paper and glue.

2 Once any painted decoration is dry, bend the large piece of construction paper into a loop and stick the edges together using double-sided tape. (Regular tape will work just as well.)

HOW IT WORKS

GETTING A LIFT

In flight, four main forces affect airplanes: lift (upward force), thrust (propulsive force), weight (gravity's pull), and drag (air resistance). The design of the wing is one of the major factors that influence lift. Air moves faster over the curved top of an airplane wing than its flatter underside. This reduces air pressure and produces lift.

STAYING ALOFT

Although a hoop glider doesn't have airplane-shaped wings, its curved hoops produce differences in air pressure that enable it to fly. After the glider is thrust forward, air speeds over the top of the hoops. The hoops' paper-thin edges create little forward drag, while their wide surfaces push down on the air, which pushes back up with an equal and opposite force. This generates lift for your glider.

Lift

Drag

Weight

Forward motion

4 Using double-sided tape, stick the loops to either end of two straws. Place two or three paperclips at the base of the smaller loop, to add weight to your hoop glider.

3

Bend the smaller piece of construction paper into a loop and secure the edges with tape. Next, stick on the two small steering vane pieces—one on either side of the loop.

IN OUR GALAXY...

GLIDING HIGH

Gliders are aircraft without engines, which gain lift from their wings and fly using air currents. They are lightweight and sleek, designed to travel through the air with as little air resistance (called drag) as possible.

SPACE GLIDERS

NASA's space shuttles used rocket engines to lift off into space, but returned to Earth as gliders. They had to be flown back to NASA piggyback on specially designed shuttle-carrier aircraft.

Anakin flies a speedy Zephyr-G swoop bike across Tatooine in search of his mother.

5

Cut out the scout trooper from black paper using the template. Fold the middle bar as shown above, then place it between the glider's straws. Tape the middle bar to the base of both straws.

6

Grasp the center of the straws and throw your speeder bike. It should glide through the air! You may want to try adding another paperclip or two in order to get the best flight.

YOU'VE DONE IT!

HOTH SNOW GLOBE

CREATE A FEARSOME WAMPA SCENE

The frozen planet Hoth is cold... very cold! The huge wampa creatures that live there are covered in thick fur for warmth. They prowl across the frozen planet in search of food, which they drag to their underground lairs. Using water, glycerin, clay, and a jar, you can build your own wampa and its icy, snow-filled cave.

WHAT YOU NEED

Jar

Polymer clay

Glycerin

Jug of water

Teaspoon

Scissors

Felt

Strong glue

Snow globe snow or glitter

Sequins

Baking tray

Oven gloves

You will also need an oven.

IN A GALAXY FAR, FAR AWAY....

Though the planet Hoth has limited wildlife, the fearsome wampa manages to survive by inhabiting underground caves. The wampa's white fur helps it blend into the snowy white landscape and allows it to sneak up on unsuspecting prey during snowstorms.

Clay icicles decorate the snow globe cave. What else could you add?

Snow globe snow scatters really well, while glitter could add some sparkle.

Felt decorated with sequins.

"THERE ISN'T ENOUGH LIFE ON THIS ICE CUBE TO FILL A SPACE CRUISER!"
Han Solo about Hoth

START HERE

1

Use polymer clay to make an icy-looking base for your wampa to stand on. It should be smaller than the jar lid. Check the jar can still close once the base is in place.

2

Create your wampa, piece by piece, out of white clay and decorate with colored clay. Press the pieces firmly together and stand it on the base, checking that the jar fits over the top.

COLD AS ICE

Luke Skywalker is caught by surprise when a wampa attacks him on Hoth. The wampa drags Luke back to its icy lair and hangs him upside down from the cave ceiling. Luke nearly becomes the wampa's next meal.

Be patient. Drying can take a few hours.

5

Place the jar lid on a flat surface. Use strong glue to attach the base and wampa to the inside of the lid. Make sure it stays upright and then leave to completely dry.

⚠

6

Fill the jar with water, almost to the top. Bottled or distilled water is better than tap water, which has impurities that can cloud the water. Then add a teaspoon or two of glycerin and stir.

3

Remember to wear oven gloves!

Lay the base and the wampa figure onto a baking tray. Bake them as directed on the polymer clay packaging. Ask an adult for help using the oven.

4

Ask an adult to apply strong glue for you.

Once they've cooled down, stick the wampa figure to the base using strong glue. Make sure the two pieces are firmly stuck together and leave to dry for a few minutes.

A troop of rebel fighters trek across the frozen wastes of Hoth on its way to the Rebel Alliance's secret headquarters, Echo Base.

7

Add glitter or snow globe snow to the jar. If it all sinks to the bottom very quickly, you may need to add a bit more glycerin. Add it slowly, testing each time until the snow floats gently.

8

Apply strong glue around the inner edge of the jar lid, then secure the lid tightly and leave to dry. If the jar leaks when you turn it over, use more glue to seal the lid from the outside.

9

Cut a strip of felt for the base of your snow globe, which will hide the jar lid. Decorate it with sequins, felt, or glitter in snowy or icy colors, and then glue it firmly around the jar lid.

10

Your snow globe is complete. Gently shake it or hold it upside down for a few seconds, then place it the right way up on a flat surface and watch it snow!

YOU'VE DONE IT!

HOW IT WORKS

VERY VISCOUS

Gravity pulls particles through liquids at different speeds, depending on the viscosity of the liquids. The more viscous (thicker) a liquid is, the more slowly particles fall through it.

SLOW FALL

Glycerin is more viscous than water. Adding glycerin to water increases the water's viscosity, slowing the downward movement of small particles such as glitter.

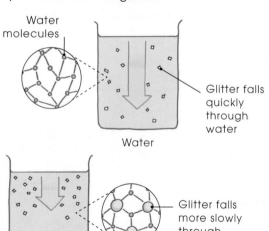

Water molecules

Glitter falls quickly through water

Water

Glitter falls more slowly through water containing glycerin

Water + glycerin

HEAT AND DUST

The scorching heat and harsh desert landscape of Tatooine means that very few people live here. The planet has become known as a refuge for scavengers, criminals, smugglers, and misfits.

Gold glitter for swirling sand.

IN OUR GALAXY...

TYPES OF PAINT

When painters brush or roll paint onto walls, they often choose paints that are highly viscous so they won't drip down the wall before they dry. Spray painting is a different story: the paint is often watered down until it has a low enough viscosity to move easily through the narrow parts of a spray painting machine.

C-3PO and R2-D2 spend a lot of time on Tatooine—as do Han Solo, Luke, and Jabba the Hutt.

WHY NOT TRY?
Tatooine's desert climate is as different from Hoth as you can get. You could re-create a raging Tatooine sandstorm using gold glitter!

TEMPLATES

These templates will help you make many of the projects in this book. Follow the instructions on page 7 on how to trace and cut out the shapes you need from these templates. You may need to enlarge the size of some templates using a photocopier to suit your needs.

■ **SUPER SPEEDER BIKE** pages 110–113

Steering vanes: 2 pieces (flip one over to make the right and left vanes)

SCORING

When using these templates it is useful to score your cardboard before you fold it. To do this, run a ballpoint pen that has run out of ink along the edge of a ruler using the dashed line on the template (see key) as a guide. It is important to fold all your scored lines before you glue or tape any of the pieces.

KEY

——	Cut line
——	Draw line (for decorating)
- - - -	Score line (for folding)
▨	Tab

stick this bit to the droid body

stick this bit to the droid body

Attachments: 2 pieces

stick attachment here

stick wheel here

stick wheel here

stick wheel here

stick wheel here

stick attachment here

■ **BUSY WORKER DROIDS** pages 38–43

Enlarge template to fit your brush.

Wheels: 4 pieces

■ GLIDING SPEEDER

pages 56–61

Speeder sides: 2 pieces (flip one over to make the right and left sides of the speeder)

Cockpit part 1
(page 76, step 9)

Stick to
pod support

■ SPEEDY PODRACERS

pages 72–77

Stick to
pod base

Cockpit part 2
(page 76,
step 9)

Tape straw
piece here

Hole for
small bendy
thumb straw

■ ANAKIN'S MECHNO-ARM

pages 50–55

Stick
cardboard
tube here

Engine support
(page 74, step 6)

Stick
cardboard
tube here

Pod support
(page 75, step 7)

Pod base
(page 76, step 9)

Stick to
cockpit part 1

Stick pilot here

Fold and stick
to opposite
flap to create
pod base

Stick to
back of
podracer

Pilot
(page 76, step 9)

Stick to top of
pod base

The template is shown
palm side up for you to
use the mechno-arm
with your right hand.
Turn the cut out shape
over if you want to use
your left hand.

■ SPACE ROCKETS pages 92–97

Enlarge template by 35%
to fit a 1 liter plastic bottle

Slave I wings: 2 pieces
(flip one over to make the
right and left wings, page
94, step 3)

Bottle holder
(page 93, step 1)

Slave I **base**
(page 93, step 2)

INVISIBLE FORCE pages 68–71

Small cut-out piece
(page 70, step 1)

Main part of lightsaber handle
(page 70, step 1)

Slits for small
cut-out piece

GLOSSARY

IN OUR GALAXY...

2D
Two-dimensional: An object that has surface area with length and width, but no depth.

3D
Three-dimensional: An object as it appears in real life: having length, width, and depth.

3D PRINTING
Using a special printing machine to build three-dimensional objects.

ACID
A sour-tasting chemical that can damage metal and other substances. Lemon juice and vinegar are common acids.

AIR RESISTANCE
A force that acts on objects when they move through air. It is caused by air molecules pushing back.

ARRAY
An arrangement of a group of similar things.

ATMOSPHERE
The layer of air around Earth.

ATOM
The basic building block for all matter in the universe.

ATTRACTION
A force that pulls things together.

BATTERY
A device used to store electrical energy.

BOND
An attracting force that holds together tiny particles such as atoms and molecules.

CARBON DIOXIDE
A mix of oxygen and carbon found as a gas in the air around us. We breathe it out as a waste product.

CASTER
A small wheel that turns freely, and is used to support and move furniture.

CHARGE
A basic characteristic of matter that has two forms: positive and negative. The force exerted between positive and negative charges holds matter together.

CHEMICAL REACTION
The transformation of one or more substances into something else. For example, when iron rusts after it is exposed to air—that's a chemical reaction.

CIRCUIT
A complete and closed path, around which an electric current can flow.

COMPRESS
To squash.

COMPOSITE MATERIAL
A composite is when two or more different materials are combined to create a new material.

CONDUCTOR
A substance through which heat or electricity can easily pass.

CROSSLINK
A bond that connects two or more polymer chains together.

CRYSTAL
A regular arrangement of atoms or molecules held together by bonds in a solid.

CYBERNETICS
The study of how to control and communicate between a living creature and a machine.

DRAG
A force that pushes against objects as they move through air or water. It is caused by air or water molecules getting in the way.

ELASTIC ENERGY
The potential energy that an object stores when it is not in motion.

ELECTRICITY
A flow of energy that carries an electrical charge.

ELECTRON
A tiny particle inside an atom that has a negative electrical charge.

ELEMENT
A substance made of one type of atom that cannot be broken down into a simpler substance by chemical reactions.

ENERGY
A physical property that can be transformed into work or motion. Energy has various forms, such as chemical energy, elastic energy, and kinetic energy (movement).

FORCE
A push or a pull between objects.

FREEZING POINT
The temperature at which water turns to ice.

GRAVITY
An attracting force between two objects. Earth's gravity keeps you firmly on the ground.

GYROSCOPE
A wheel mounted to spin rapidly about an axis that is free to turn in various directions.

INSULATE
To protect something from the flow of electricity, heat, or sound.

KINETIC ENERGY
The energy of motion.

LIGHT WAVES
A form of energy that we perceive as light.

MAGNETIC FIELD
The area around a magnet in which magnetic material will be attracted or repelled.

MINERAL
A natural material from the Earth's crust. There are hundreds of different types. Rocks are made of minerals.

MOLECULE
Two or more atoms held together by bonds.

OXYGEN
An element. One of the gases in air, essential for most of the life on Earth.

PARTICLE
A tiny bit of matter, such as an atom or molecule.

PHOTOVOLTAIC
A technology that captures and converts energy from the sun into electricity. Photovoltaic cells are commonly used in solar panels.

PLASMA
Plasma is a gas where some or all of its electrons have separated from the atoms. It is made up of positively and negatively charged particles.

PNEUMATIC
Containing, or operated by, pressurized air or gas.

POLYETHYLENE
A tough, light, flexible plastic, used to make plastic bags.

POLYMER
A long chain of similar molecules.

PRESSURE
The force that one area of a gas, liquid, or solid exerts on another.

REPULSION
A force that pushes things away from each other.

ROBOTICS
A specialized branch of technology that focuses on the design, construction, operation, and application of robots.

SEMICONDUCTING MATERIAL
A material that is a poor conductor at low temperatures, but that can conduct more electricity when heat or light is added.

SOLUTION
A mixture of two or more chemicals, normally a solid, which has dissolved into a liquid.

SUPERSATURATED
A supersaturated solution is one that contains more of a substance, such as sugar, than can be completely dissolved.

STATIC ELECTRICITY
The build up of electric charge on an object that has lost or gained electrons.

SYNTHETIC
A material or chemical that is made by combining different artificial substances.

THRUST
A pushing force.

THRUSTER
Part of a vehicle that pushes it forward.

VISCOSITY
The property of a liquid that describes how fast or slow it will flow. A thick, sticky substance, such as honey, flows more slowly than water because it has a high viscosity.

VISCOUS
Having a high viscosity.

VULCANIZED RUBBER
Rubber that is treated by a chemical or physical process, such as heating, in order to improve the rubber's strength or elasticity.

IN A GALAXY FAR, FAR AWAY....

BOUNTY HUNTER
Someone who is paid to find or destroy people or objects.

DROIDS
Mechanical beings possessed with artificial intelligence, which perform tasks considered too lowly, dangerous, or complex for living species.

FIRST ORDER
A political and military faction made up of Imperial officers, nobles, and scientists who had survived the fall of the once-great Galactic Empire.

GALACTIC EMPIRE
The powerful and corrupt dictatorship that ruled most of the Galaxy through fear, until it was defeated by the Rebel Alliance.

JEDI
A Force-attuned person who uses the light side of the Force for good.

MANDIBLES
Long arms that jut out from the front of a spaceship.

REPULSORLIFT
A way of raising a vehicle off the ground using thrust.

REBEL ALLIANCE
A group of heroes who fight against the evil Galactic Empire.

RESISTANCE
A small, secret military force formed and led by General Leia Organa to combat the First Order.

SITH
An ancient sect of Force-attuned people who seek to use the dark side of the Force to gain power.

THE FORCE
An energy that flows through all living things. It can be used for good or evil.

TRACTOR BEAM
An invisible force field or energy beam that can move objects in space.

Senior Editors Cefn Ridout, Elizabeth Dowsett
Senior Designer Clive Savage
Project Editors Shari Last, Katy Lennon
Designer Rosamund Bird
Pre-production Producer Marc Staples
Senior Producer Zara Markland
Managing Editor Sadie Smith
Managing Art Editor Vicky Short
DTP Designers Satish Gaur, Rajdeep Singh
Publisher Julie Ferris
Art Director Lisa Lanzarini
Publishing Director Simon Beecroft

DK would like to thank: Brett Rector, Leland Chee, Matt Martin, Pablo Hidalgo, and Michael Siglain at Lucasfilm; Chelsea Alon at Disney Publishing; Lol Johnson for photography; Henry Mulhall for photography assistance; Jenny Edwards for additional photography; Jemma Westing and Anna Sander for making the models; Jon Hall for the science illustrations; Andy Bishop and Anne Sharples for design assistance; Nicola Torode and UL VS Ltd for safety consultancy; Darren Matthews at the Centre for Literacy in Primary Education for education consultancy; Clive Gifford for science consultancy; Alexandra Beeden for proofreading; Clara Afram, Pamela Afram, Bettie Capstick, Lola Capstick, Akiko Kato, Rebecca Pitt, Gema Salamanca, Jack Whyte, Archie Whitehead, and Abi Wright for modeling.

First American Edition, 2018
Published in the United States by DK Publishing
345 Hudson Street, New York, New York 10014

Page design copyright © 2018 Dorling Kindersley Limited
DK, a Division of Penguin Random House LLC
18 19 20 21   10 9 8 7 6 5 4 3 2 1
001–307684–July/2018

© & TM 2018 LUCASFILM LTD.

A catalog record for this book is available from the Library of Congress.

ISBN 978-1-4654-6712-6

DK books are available at special discounts when purchased in bulk for sales promotions, premiums, fund-raising, or educational use. For details, contact: DK Publishing SpecialMarkets, 345 Hudson Street, New York, New York 10014 SpecialSales@dk.com

Printed and bound in China

A WORLD OF IDEAS:
SEE ALL THERE IS TO KNOW
www.dk.com
www.starwars.com

The publisher would like to thank the following for their kind permission to reproduce their photographs:
(Key: a-above; b-below/bottom; c-centre; f-far; l-left; r-right; t-top)

11 Dreamstime.com: Tamas Bedecs (br). 17 NASA: (clb). 23 iStockphoto.com: urosmm (br). 29 NASA: (br). 35 Depositphotos Inc: ewastudio (br). 49 Dreamstime.com: Pablo Hidalgo / Pxhidalgo (br). 55 Courtesy of Shadow Robot Company Ltd: (br). 59 Depositphotos Inc: muro (br). 71 Depositphotos Inc: mihtiander (br). 81 Depositphotos Inc: yothinpi (br). 91 123RF.com: Smileus (br). 95 NASA: MSFC (br). 101 Depositphotos Inc: zastavkin (tl). 111 Skitterphoto: Peter Heeling (br). 113 Dorling Kindersley: NASA (cr). 119 Depositphotos Inc: nrey_ad (cr)

For further information see: www.dkimages.com

Liz Lee Heinecke

Liz Lee Heinecke is a lifelong *Star Wars* fan. After gaining a master's degree in bacteriology, Liz began doing science at home with her kids, documenting their experiments on KitchenPantryScientist.com. She appears on television, makes science videos, and writes about science online and in books. Liz's other work includes *Kitchen Science Lab for Kids*, *Outdoor Science Lab for Kids*, and *STEAM Lab for Kids*.

Cole Horton

Cole Horton is an author, historian, and games industry professional. He is the co-author of multiple *Star Wars* books, including *Star Wars Absolutely Everything You Need to Know*, *Star Wars: The Visual Encyclopedia*, and *Lego Star Wars: Chronicles of the Force*. Cole lives in San Francisco with his wife. You can find him online at ColeHorton.com and on Twitter @ColeHorton.